for LIFE
CHORISTER'S COMPANION

RSCM

This book and its typography, artwork and layouts are
Copyright © 2009 The Royal School of Church Music
19 The Close, Salisbury, Wiltshire, SP1 2EB, England
Tel: +44 (0)1722 424848 Fax: +44 (0)1722 424849
E-mail: press@rscm.com Website: www.rscm.com

RSCM membership is open collectively
to churches, colleges and schools,
and individually to all interested in church music.

Choirboy's Pocket Book
First printed 1934

The Chorister's Pocket Book
First printed 1937
Revised editions 1947, 1961 & 1967

The Chorister's Companion
First published 1980
Second edition 1989
Third edition 1995

The Voice for Life Chorister's Companion
First published 2009
Second edition 2013

All rights reserved
ISBN: 978-0-85402-169-7
Order Number: G0021
Edited by Tim Ruffer
Illustrations by Hilary Perona-Wright
Printed in Great Britain by Hobbs & Co.

CONTENTS

Contents

This little book is designed to give choristers something that will help them to understand more clearly the religious and musical aspects of their work as church musicians.

It was first published in 1934 as 'The Choirboy's Pocket Book' under the editorship of Sir Sydney Nicholson, founder and first Director of the RSCM. It was very popular and sold 140,000 copies in 45 years.

In 1980 it came out in a new edition under the title 'The Chorister's Companion'. The then Director, Dr Lionel Dakers, said in his introduction that it was necessary to bring it up to date as so much had changed in the life of the Church since the days before the Second World War when the book was first published.

Nearly thirty years later, the need for a total revision has never been greater and the church in which we now serve with our music making is almost unrecognisable from the church that Sir Sydney served.

Music is, however, still vital to the life of the church and I hope that you will enjoy using this book and that it will enable you to make the most of your musical gifts to the glory of God and to fulfil the motto of the RSCM:

I will sing with the spirit and with
the understanding also

Lindsay Gray, Director, RSCM
June 2009

From Aled Jones, singer

Singing has always been a big part of my life, from performing in local Eisteddfodau (competitive arts festivals) near my home on Anglesey, North Wales, to singing in churches, concert venues and recording studios all over the world. It's very demanding and challenging but also hugely fulfilling. I love to sing; I always have done and always will.

Something I learnt when very young is the importance of giving of one's best, whether to a congregation of a handful of people, or to a packed building with standing room only. There have been many occasions, both happy and sad, when quite clearly the music meant so much to those present, in ways which the spoken word could not.

I'm thrilled to commend *The Chorister's Companion* to a new generation of singers. It will help you to serve your church or school community, and use your voice to the best of your ability. Singing is enriching and rewarding in so many different ways; not only are you the proud owner of a *Voice for Life*, but you are part of a wonderful network of musicians and colleagues worldwide for whom singing is an important part of their lives and faith.

THE SINGING CHURCH

a brief history

By Harry Bramma

Since the earliest times, there have been singers in our churches. The first Christians sang in the synagogues and naturally continued to sing when separate Christian churches were established. You will remember our Lord and His disciples sang a hymn together on the night before the Crucifixion.

It was not long before schools were attached to churches in which boys were taught singing. Indeed, in the later middle ages, the monks and teachers in monasteries and schools were largely responsible for the way in which our music in the Western World developed.

Systems of writing music were invented, people were taught to sing and small organs were built in the larger churches. Some cathedrals like Salisbury and Worcester were particularly famous for music in the 13th, 14th and 15th centuries. In all the old cathedrals and in several of the College Chapels at Oxford and Cambridge, there was a choir of gentlemen and boys, and to this day the tradition continues. People come from all over the world to hear our cathedral choirs.

One of the most famous choirs in the 16th century was the choir of the Chapels Royal. Many of the greatest composers such as Byrd, Tallis and Tomkins were associated with this choir. The choristers had an exciting life, doubling up very often as actors.

Even as late as Shakespeare's time, the principal female parts in theatres were often taken by boy choristers.

In most parish churches, there were no choirs until the middle of the 19th century and many churches did not possess an organ until around 1850. Formerly singers would have sat with the village band in the West Gallery of the Church.

After the middle of the 19th century, as a result of the influence of the Oxford Movement, the appearance of our Parish Churches began to change dramatically. High box pews were removed, and the organ and choir were placed in front of the congregation in the chancel. It was at this time that choirs of men and boys became a regular part of the life of most churches. Over the past hundred years thousands of boys and girls have passed through the choirs. Many have come to learn and love music simply because one day they chanced to join a church choir.

In the later 19th century, many new Roman Catholic Churches were built and these too quite often had a choir of men and boys. In the Free Churches (Methodists, Baptists, Congregationalists) the singing was usually led by a mixed choir of adults who sat in a gallery on either side of the organ at the front of the church.

Nowadays in our churches there are many boy and girl choristers. They continue to do marvellous work in leading the praises of the Church. They also have a difficult job. Singing is the only skilled activity in

which children and adults take part together on equal
terms. The top line of the music sung by trebles and
sopranos has to be just as well done as the lower parts
sung by the altos, tenors and basses.

As you can see from this brief historical survey,
choristers are part of a movement which goes back to
the earliest days of the Church – indeed to the time of
Jesus Christ himself. Choristers should be proud they
are continuing a tradition which started so long ago;
they must also be thrilled to know that through their
love and enjoyment of music and through their ability
to sing really well, they are able to inspire and lead the
worship of the Christian family at their local church,
of which their choir is a significant part.

'The world is full of people,

each with God-given abilities...'

THE ROLE OF THE CHORISTER

A God-given voice for life

By Leah Perona-Wright

God creates each person with natural talents and gifts, and with unique personalities. The Psalmist describes how God carefully plans every intricate detail of our lives: 'You created my inmost being; you knit me together in my mother's womb' (*Psalm 139:13*)

The world is full of people, each with different kinds of God-given abilities; great thinkers, inventors, teachers, explorers, athletes, and creative types like artists, writers and musicians to name only a few. But there are other important kinds of gifts too – like being able to listen, to be generous, or to offer friendship and kindness to others. 'There are different kinds of spiritual gifts, but they all come from the same Spirit. There are different ways to serve the same Lord, and we can each do different things. Yet the same God works in all of us and helps us in everything we do.' (*1 Corinthians 12: 4–6, Contemporary English Version*) If you are a chorister then you have already discovered that you have a musical talent – your singing voice is a precious God-given gift.

As Christians we each have a responsibility to try and develop our God-given abilities and we offer these gradually improving and developing gifts to God throughout our lives for His pleasure and glory. As a chorister, you offer your musical gifts in service to God and to others in your church. You have a really important job to do, and will already be making an extremely important contribution to the musical worship at your church or school.

But you may also find that God calls you to use your musical gifts in other ways too – perhaps brightening up somebody's Christmas by carol singing at a local retirement home, or singing for a fund-raising concert, or forming new friendships by making music in choirs or orchestras outside your school or church. It is certain that your musical talent will bring joy to many people throughout your life. It will also bring great pleasure to God as He sees you hone your ability and use it for His glory.

> To serve others through music is a joyful calling that requires hard work but also brings great rewards. We should always try and give the best we can, and we must constantly try to improve our standards of singing and our understanding of what we are singing and why.

INTRODUCING VOICE FOR LIFE

+ Do you long to develop your God-given musical ability?

+ Would you like to feel more confident about your singing and strengthen your voice?

+ Do you need more confidence with musical skills like sight-singing or aural (listening)?

+ Do you understand what the purpose of your choir is, and how you fit into this?

+ Could you take more responsibility within the choir to help other less experienced members?

+ Do you like to know how you are getting on in the choir, and how you can be promoted to a more senior and responsible position?

The *Voice for Life* training scheme is designed to help you discover what your voice can do, and then strengthen it. It will also help you to improve your knowledge and understanding of music, and help you look at what it means to be a singer and member of a choir. As you work through the training scheme you will find your voice develops and changes and you will improve as a musician and choir member. This is rewarding in itself, but you will also be able to see your own progress throughout the scheme, with your achievements being acknowledged and rewarded.

How does it work?

There are five levels in the *Voice for Life* scheme, for singers of any age from beginners through to advanced singers, starting with a preparatory level for brand new, inexperienced singers:

White (preparatory level)

Light Blue

Dark Blue

Red

Yellow

The preparatory *White Level* for brand new singers (i.e. probationers/trainee choir members) covers the absolute basics that any singer in a choir should know. The resources for the *White Level* are available for download on the RSCM website, and there is a *White Record Card* available for purchase which lists the targets to be worked on with space to sign and date each one as it is achieved.

On completion of this preparatory level, you are admitted as a 'full member of the choir' and there is an RSCM 'admission to the choir' certificate that can be given to mark this special occasion. There is also a *Voice for Life* White certificate and lapel badge that can be awarded to formally acknowledge your achievement.

Once you have become a full member of the choir, you move on to the four main levels of *Voice for Life*: Light Blue, Dark Blue, Red and Yellow.

Each level of *Voice for Life* has clear targets which state exactly what you need to achieve or demonstrate, to be awarded the next level. These are listed in the back of the *Voice for Life* Singer's Workbooks with a space for your choir trainer or teacher to sign and date each target as it is achieved, showing your progress through that level. At *White Level* the targets are listed on a special *Record Card*.

Once you have completed the necessary training for that level, reached the targets and finished your workbook, you may be awarded your RSCM *Voice for Life* medal and the appropriately coloured ribbon (for robed choirs) or coloured lapel badge for non-robed choirs. You then move on to the next level.

What skills will I work on and improve?

At each level of *Voice for Life* you will work on improving your skills and understanding in five different areas (or 'Modules'):

MODULE A: Using the voice well

In this module you will learn how to use your voice in a healthy way, for example, to make sure you have the strength and stamina to sing through a long rehearsal or service without straining your voice. You will also develop your understanding of what is happening physically when you sing so that you can learn how to look after your voice and how to make the best use of it.

MODULE B: Musical skills and understanding

As a choir member you will already be aware of the importance of being able to learn new music as quickly and confidently as possible. This involves skills like being able to follow the music; using your ears as well as understanding the music you are looking at on the page.

This module will help develop your knowledge of musical notes and rhythms, musical terms, and will help improve your listening skills. All this will enable you to join in confidently with the music you sing in your choir, but gradually over time as your skills improve, you will be able to help lead the other singers in the choir when learning and performing new music.

MODULE C: Repertoire

Why do you think a song or anthem has words? As a singer, your job is to decide what the message of your song or anthem is and then communicate this as clearly as you can when you perform the music to your listeners. You will learn to do this by thinking about the meaning of the words that you sing, and the mood and style of the music itself. This module will make sure you are aware of why you are singing, what you are singing, and what you are singing about.

Through the earthquake, wind and fire

O still small voice of calm

MODULE D: Belonging to the choir

As a choir member, you need to work on your own vocal skills in order to be the best singer you can, aiming to be a good influence and example to others in your choir. You need to be reliable, cooperative and committed, as well as the best singer and musician you possibly can.

However, being a good example in a choir also means recognising that you are part of a team. It is important to contribute to the well being of the team as a whole. This means being aware of the other members of the choir. Are you helpful to the less experienced singers? Are you able to be encouraging when someone else is given a solo, rather than feeling jealous that you were not asked to sing it this time around? Do you notice when a new or shy member of the choir needs looking after or befriending?

MODULE E: Choir in context

What is your choir for? What is its purpose? The choir is a team or community in its own right, but it is also part of a wider community – a church or a school, village or town. If you are part of a church choir, you will be 'leading' the congregation in their musical worship, but you need to remember that you are also part of the congregation, not a separate entity. You need to see yourself as part of the whole church.

When you finish singing for a service it is good to ask yourself whether you were really engaged in the service or whether you just switched-off as soon as you finished singing. Did you really manage to pray? Did you listen to God's word? This module reminds us that as a chorister in a choir, we have an important job to do, but we are also an important part of a wider family/community.

You will gradually work on these five different areas, improving your skills and knowledge and working your way through the training scheme.

General progress and weekly standards

Your general progress will be easy to see as it will be recorded in the back of your Singer's Workbook (or record card at the White Level), with your choir trainer or teacher gradually signing off the targets as you achieve each one. Your choir trainer may also choose to use a General Progress Chart to record in outline each singer's progress through the scheme. This will probably be displayed somewhere prominent, on your vestry or rehearsal room wall.

Your choir trainer may also use a Weekly Standards Chart to show the level of consistency of your singing and general contribution at each rehearsal and service. If the Weekly Standards Chart is used you will be part of a 'Team' within your choir, and there may be team competitions. However, ideally the need to learn new music and perform well should supply the necessary incentive for everyone to work hard.

Positions of responsibility

In addition to working your way through the *Voice for Life* levels, your choir trainer may choose to give particular members of the choir special areas of responsibility. For you to be trusted with one of these special roles you would have to demonstrate a consistently good standard of work and reliability. These roles may include:

Head Chorister (or Choir Captain)

Team Leader

It may be a disappointment if you are not chosen for one of these roles. You need to show the right qualities though – it is not just a question of having been in the choir for a long time, or being the eldest member of the choir. Are you a good influence and example to the other singers? Are you supportive of the choir trainer at all times?

If you are appointed Head Chorister you may be given a special medal or badge. You can wear this in place of your *Voice for Life* medal on whichever coloured ribbon you have currently reached in the *Voice for Life* scheme.

If you have been appointed as Head Chorister of your choir, have a look at pages 87-89 as this will give you some tips and ideas on how to be the best Head Chorister you possibly can.

Other RSCM singing awards

In addition to the *Voice for Life* levels which are assessed informally by your own choir trainer or teacher, the RSCM also offers an optional complementary system of singing awards at three levels: Bronze, Silver and Gold.

These are assessed by a formal singing examination. The syllabuses for these awards are based on the same five skills areas (or modules) as the *Voice for Life* levels. They have been designed to fit in with the *Voice for Life* training scheme so that you can progress gradually through the levels as follows:

White

Light Blue

Dark Blue

BRONZE

Red

SILVER

Yellow

GOLD

The Bronze, Silver and Gold examinations are optional awards for which your choir trainer can choose to enter singers in order to affirm the standards being achieved informally within the choir on the *Voice for Life* training scheme. Like the *Voice for Life* levels, the Bronze, Silver and Gold awards are open to singers of any age.

For more information on the *Voice for Life* materials, the Bronze, Silver and Gold examinations and to download a copy of the award syllabuses go to the RSCM website: www.rscm.com

The RSCM medals and badges

Voice for Life medal

Head Chorister medal

Bronze, Silver & Gold Award medal design

The RSCM medals and badges

The medals with appropriately coloured ribbon and the lapel badges are awarded to mark your achievement as you progress through the *Voice for Life* training scheme. They are not there purely for decoration and will not be given out simply because you have been in the choir for a long time. Try to remember:

- **Medals/badges are only symbols**
  Much more important than the medal or badge is the possession by you of the right attitude and level of competence.

- **Badges and all 'symbols of office' (e.g. Head Chorister medals) should not draw attention to themselves**
  They are first of all a reminder to the bearer of responsibility and the need for service.

- **The wearing of more than one medal/ribbon is strongly discouraged**
  Only the most senior or most relevant badge/medal should be displayed at any one time.

x   **✓**

The wearing of more than one
medal/ribbon is strongly discouraged

USING THE VOICE WELL

Singing is a physical activity which requires energy, strength, stamina, concentration and dedication.

Sportsmen and women need regular training and exercise in order to perform to the best of their ability. Sprinters would not only spend their time running 100 metre races – they have a gruelling fitness regime in order to improve their general fitness level and strengthen their muscles. If they only appeared at a competition to compete in the 100 metre sprint with little or no training beforehand, they would be in serious danger of pulling a muscle or doing some other kind of physical damage. They would certainly not run the race to the best of their ability.

Like sport, singing requires regular training and exercise in order to keep all the muscles and vocal functions strong. The whole body is involved in singing – your body is your musical instrument. This means that how you stand or sit will affect your singing voice. If you feel tired, stressed or unwell you will notice a difference in how your voice works. Even what we eat can affect how well the voice works!

This section of the book will give you some ideas about how you can look after your voice and body, and how you can get the best out of your singing voice.

Remember to look in your *Voice for Life* Singer's Workbook – this is full of helpful tips and advice on looking after your voice, and gives lots of vocal exercises you can use to strengthen and improve your singing.

Standing and sitting to sing

Standing and sitting to sing

When standing to sing you should have:

- A tall posture with a straight back and upright head
- Your weight distributed evenly on both feet
- Relaxed knees
- Relaxed shoulders
- Your feet slightly apart and firmly on the ground

Generally, it is better to stand than sit while singing, but if you have a good posture you can still sing well while sitting. You should aim to have:

- An upright posture
- Relaxed shoulders
- A straight back
- Both feet firmly on the ground

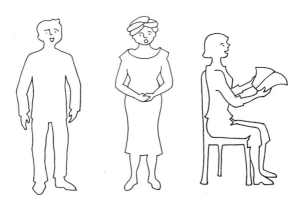

If your posture is not good you will find that tension creeps into various muscles in your body. This will start to affect your singing voice making your voice feel tight and tired.

The way you hold your music will affect your posture. If you hold your music too high, it will cover your mouth. Too low, and the sound will go straight down to the floor. Either way you will not be able to see your conductor properly and your congregation or audience will not be able to see or hear you well.

You will know when you are holding your music at the right height, as you will be able to see your conductor over the top of your music without needing to move your head (you can just move your eyes).

As well as affecting the voice, the way you stand or sit also makes a visual impression on the people you are singing for. Your posture or body language can tell your congregation or audience that you are relaxed and confident, or that you are frightened or even bored.

A singer or choir that stands well will create a positive impact before they even begin to sing – they look focused and professional. This helps the congregation or audience to relax and enjoy the music with confidence. Keep this in mind when you are singing!

Remember: Good posture will allow your voice to work to the best of its ability and also creates a good impression on your congregation or audience. Always try and remember to stand or sit well throughout your rehearsals, performances and services.

Breathing

Breathing is a natural reflex. This means that in normal life you do not have to think about it – it happens automatically. However, when you sing, you do need to think about breathing because you need to breathe in a different way, with more control. Your breathing affects all aspects of your voice including the tone (or sound) of your singing voice, your dynamics (the louds and softs), and your tuning. Learning to control your breathing, increasing your breath capacity and breathing in the right places will all help make sense of the words and music you sing.

When breathing to sing, you need to learn to:

- Take in deeper breaths
- Control the outward breath
- Breathe in the right places in the music to make sense of the words and musical phrases
- Keep the chest, shoulders and throat relaxed!

Use the exercises in your Singer's Workbook to help improve your breathing technique, and remember that good posture is important in keeping your breathing relaxed and free. You might also like to try the following exercises:

Relaxed shoulders and throat

To remind yourself that you need to keep relaxed shoulders and throat when breathing, try lying down on the floor on your back. Breathe in and out deeply and make a mental note of how relaxed your shoulders and throat are. Then stand up, breathe in and out deeply again, and try to get the same level of relaxation in your shoulders and throat again.

 Controlling the breath with a hiss

Breathe in slowly to a count of 4 beats (making sure your shoulders and throat stay completely relaxed). Hold for 4 beats and breathe out over a count of 4 hissing like a snake or a kettle letting off steam. Now try again, keeping your inward count at 4 and your holding count at 4, but increasing the number of counts you breathe out over to 6, then 8, then 10 or more if you can manage it!

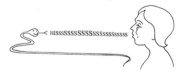

Controlling the breath with a hum

As before, breathe in slowly over a count of 4 beats (keeping your shoulders and throat relaxed). Hold for 4 beats and then hum a fairly low note in your range for a count of 4 beats. Each time you repeat the exercise, increase the number of counts that you hum to, keeping the tone and the volume as even as possible. You could then try the exercise again, but instead of humming on the outward counts, sing the note to a vowel like 'Oo' or 'Ah'.

Remember: Breathing affects all aspects of your singing so every singer, no matter how experienced, needs to work on their breathing and try to develop their lung capacity.

The tone and range of your voice

In your throat is the voice box or larynx. This contains your vocal folds: sound is made by breath passing through these vocal folds and making them vibrate. (If you want to know where the larynx is, put your hands or fingers gently on your throat while you speak or sing – you will feel the vibrations from your larynx. You can also feel the larynx move upwards when you swallow.)

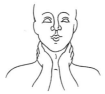

The sound that comes from the vocal folds is amplified by the throat, mouth and, to some extent, the nose as it resonates in these hollow parts of your body. You should always aim for a resonant, focused sound when you sing, and the following will help you to do this:

+ Make sure you open your mouth when you sing! Otherwise, you will trap the sound inside your mouth. Try singing in front of a mirror – most people are surprised to discover that they are not opening their mouths as wide as they think they are when they sing!

- Try and create as much space inside your mouth as possible when you sing, particularly at the back of the mouth. You might like to try yawning or imagine you are biting into a large and juicy peach – keep the tongue flat and feel the soft fleshy part at the back of your mouth (your soft palate) rising. Aim for this relaxed feeling of space when you sing.

- Keep your throat as relaxed and open as possible, and your jaw relaxed when you sing. If you tighten up your jaw or your throat then the sound will become strained or strangled.

- If you want to increase the strength and stamina of your voice so you can sing higher and lower notes in your range, and sing for longer without getting tired, you need to exercise your voice regularly. Singing once a week at choir practice will not be enough to give your singing the strength, agility and stamina that you are hoping for.

Use the exercises in your Singer's Workbook regularly at home, and take every opportunity you can to sing! Here are some other exercises you might like to use to supplement your practice at home:

Gentle warming up, and finding a forward resonant sound

Hum a long note, somewhere in the middle of your range, feeling the buzz in your nose (you might like to touch your nose when you do this at first). Now hum this note again, getting the buzz in your nose, then open onto the vowel 'ee' feeling the same buzz in your nose. When you can do this try other vowels like 'aw', 'oo' and 'ah'.

Positioning the tongue, opening the throat, finding resonance

Say the word 'Sing!' Notice how the back of your tongue is up against the roof of your mouth as you say the 'ng' part of the word. You can probably also feel your upper molar teeth with the sides of your tongue. Now try singing the 'ng' sound, then opening onto an 'ee' sound. You might also like to try other vowels like 'ng – eh', 'ng – ah', 'ng – aw', and 'ng – oo'.

Increasing range

Starting on a comfortable note in your range, make a sliding/siren sound – slide from this note up to a higher note and back down again. (You can do this using an 'ng' sound, a 'hum' or any vowel of your choice.) Make sure the tone is even and the notes are smoothly connected. When you can do this you can gradually increase the distance between the notes, creating a longer slide/siren.

Remember: Your voice needs to be treated like a sportsman or woman treats their body. You need to give your voice regular exercise and training in order to keep your singing as strong and agile as possible.

Words

Usually when you sing you will sing more than just music – there will be words too. These words have been set to the music for a reason. As a singer, your job is to communicate these words to your listener. This means you need to make them as clear and expressive as possible. The way you pronounce and express your words is called 'diction'.

Very often your listeners (whether a congregation at church or concert audience) do not have the words you are singing in front of them. This means they are totally relying on your diction being as clear as possible so that they can hear and understand what you are singing about.

When you sing, you need to open your mouth more than when you speak in order for the words and sound to project. You also have to use more energy than you might think with your tongue, lips and teeth to pronounce all the sounds as clearly as possible. To get your mouth moving during your own practice, try singing some tongue twisters.

 ### Exercising your mouth

Sing these tongue twisters (or any tongue twister of your choice) to a scale pattern making the words as clear as possible.

Red lorry, yellow lorry
Copper bottomed coffee pot
Tip of the tongue and the lips and the teeth

Words are made up of vowels and consonants. You should aim to make your vowel sounds as bright and resonant as possible, and your consonants as clear and crisp as possible. To practise projecting consonants try the following exercise:

 Projecting consonants

Choose a song or hymn that you know well. Whisper the words with as much energy as you can imagining that you are trying to make the words heard and understood by someone at the other side of the room. Then sing the song or hymn quietly, but with the consonants as loud and clear as you can. This may feel strange at first, but will make sure your consonants are audible and clear for your listeners. Note how much energy you are using for your consonants here, and aim to sing with this amount of energy all the time.

 Remember: When you sing, ask yourself if your listeners can hear and understand what you are singing about. The words have been set to music for a reason and it is your job to communicate them!

Looking after your voice

As your voice is part of your body, how you feel physically affects your singing voice. When a singer catches a cold or gets over-tired or stressed, they can lose their voice, which means that their musical instrument (the voice) does not work until the body recovers to full health. This is extremely frustrating, but just goes to show how important it is for a singer to look after their body in order to keep the voice healthy. In addition to physical illness, there are a surprising number of other things which can affect how your voice works, ranging from how tired you are to what you eat.

Here are some tips to help you look after your voice:

+ Tiredness affects your voice, as it takes more effort to breathe and speak, leading to vocal strain. Tiredness also makes your throat drier, which makes the voice sound strained and lacking in resonance. Make sure you get plenty of rest before you sing!

+ Did you know that you need to be reasonably fit to sing well? To help improve your stamina for singing, consider taking some form of regular exercise. Running, cycling, aerobics or swimming are all good forms of aerobic exercise, but there are many other sporting activities that will help to keep your heart and lungs healthy. Anything that keeps you active for around 20 minutes is good.

- Give yourself a good vocal workout regularly. Even if you can only manage a short practice session of 5–10 minutes a day using the exercises in your Singer's Workbook, this will strengthen your vocal muscles so they can perform better during your rehearsals and services.

- Drink plenty of water. Try and drink at least half a litre of water before exercising the voice to keep your vocal cords flexible and moist. This is important for keeping your voice healthy. A singer should drink at least two litres of water a day.

- Eat little and often. This will give you stamina to sing for long periods. If you have not had a proper meal before you sing, eat an energy bar half an hour beforehand. This will keep your energy levels up during your rehearsal or performance.

- Try to avoid drinking fruit juice before a concert or service. This can make your throat feel clogged up and 'congested'. Drink water instead.

+ You may also find that dairy products like cheese, milk, chocolate, etc make you feel clogged up and 'congested' in your throat so avoid eating these immediately before singing.

+ Try not to clear your throat or cough immediately before singing. It puts the larynx (your voice box) into trauma and closes the throat just as it needs to be opened. It is much better to swallow (either with or without a drink of water) to try and clear the mucous if you can.

+ Singing should not hurt your throat. If your throat feels sore when you sing, stop and have a rest. You almost certainly have tension creeping in somewhere in your body, and may be trying to sing notes that are too high or too low for you. Ask your choir trainer for advice, and consider taking a short course of singing lessons to help you with this problem. Remember that if you only sing once a week at choir practice your voice will tire much more quickly than if you exercise your voice more regularly.

Remember: Your voice is part of your body. If you are tired, stressed, or unwell, your voice will suffer. Look after yourself to ensure a healthy voice!

Boys' changing voices

One of the most exciting stages for a young man who loves singing is the time when his voice begins to change. For some singers this change will be gradual, for others it could appear to happen very quickly and come as a surprise.

How do I know that my voice is changing?

These are developments you may notice:

- Sudden height gain

- The quality of your speaking voice alters (this may be pointed out by people you speak to regularly on the telephone).

- You are able to sing more lower notes than before.

- You are now finding that notes around the middle of your range do not have the same qualities or are not singable.

- The top of your range is now more difficult.

- Your speaking voice cracks occasionally and you feel embarrassed about this.

- Increased variability in your singing, more 'off' days.

Firstly, DO NOT WORRY! Although these are some of the likely symptoms of a changing voice, it could be months before you can no longer sing notes in the treble range, or it might be just a few weeks.

> There are likely to be occasions when you can sing with ease and occasions when your voice does not work in the way you expect. You are going to go through a season of new discoveries as your voice settles. This is entirely normal and should be enjoyed.

What do I do with my developing voice?
If you are sensible and sing only the range of notes that are comfortable during this changing period you can continue to enjoy singing. If you continue singing sensibly, even while your voice is changing, the co-ordination in the vocal muscles will begin to develop, enabling you to sing well for the rest of your life.

What part should I be singing in the choir?
Once you have found your secure singing range it will give you a guide for which part is the most appropriate for you at the moment. While your voice is changing it is safest to sing the lowest comfortable part. It is quite possible that you will move from alto to tenor to bass within a relatively short period of time (a year or so). You may then find that your range increases to enable you to move back to tenor or maybe even to alto. However, every voice is unique. Don't worry if your progress is different from others.

Girls' developing voices

As the female voice matures, there is a transition from a sweet, delicate sound to a stronger, richer sound, with a greater contrast of tone and colour.

What do I do with my developing voice?

As your voice develops, the resonating areas can increase in size. This changes the quality of the tone. These changes should be interpreted cautiously. For example, if you develop warmer tones in the lower part of your voice, don't think you should automatically be an alto as this may result in you not developing your upper range and reaching your full potential as a soprano.

It is important that you do not compare your volume of sound with another singer of the same age because you may be developing at a different rate. Like an athlete, technique needs to be consolidated over a long period in order to achieve and sustain excellence.

When singing in a choir it is important to use the whole range of the voice regularly. If you are normally a soprano, try singing second soprano and alto parts as well. Equally, if you normally sing alto, have a go at singing the higher parts. Singing and swapping parts is also very good for building greater confidence in sight-singing.

MUSICAL SKILLS AND UNDERSTANDING

As a choir member you will already be aware of the importance of being able to learn new music as quickly and confidently as possible. This involves skills such as being able to follow the music; using your ears as well as understanding the musical shapes and terms you are looking at on the page. As you improve these skills it will enable you to join in confidently with the music you sing in your choir and then to lead the other singers in the choir when learning and performing new music.

Your *Voice for Life* Singer's Workbook contains lots of exercises, games and puzzles for you to complete which will help you to increase your knowledge and understanding of what you are looking at on the page and how to read music more confidently. This section of the book will offer you some additional advice on reading music and some helpful reference material to supplement your developing knowledge.

Hints and tips on reading music

Here are some hints and tips to bear in mind as you begin your journey of music reading:

* Learning to read music is like learning a new language. Most of the rules are easy to learn, but it is a skill that requires regular practice. The more you try the better you will get.

* Follow the music in every piece that you sing. Use your ears and your eyes together to try and link each sound that you hear with a note on the page. At first you may just be following the words, but then try noticing the shape of the notes above the words, and notice that when a note sounds higher than the one before, the corresponding note on the page also looks higher. This is what reading 'pitch' is all about.

* Remember to count. Your time signature will tell you how many regular beats there are in each bar. This regular beat or pulse continues throughout the piece, through the long and short notes, and even through the rests (or silences). The shape of each note on the page tells you for how many beats each individual note lasts. This is what reading 'rhythm' is all about.

+ As you progress in music reading, try reading whole bars or even whole phrases rather than just looking at the next note. It is much better to get an overall sense of the shape of the music than to get stuck or bogged down over one awkward interval.

Remember: The aim of reading music is to be able to perform new pieces. Don't feel inhibited or shy about making mistakes when singing through new music. The odd mistake doesn't matter – it is much better to keep following the music, keep going despite your mistakes and, if you have stopped, make sure you join in again with the rest of the choir as soon as you can.

SOME BASIC MUSIC THEORY

Notes of the treble clef

If you are a soprano, treble, or alto or even tenor, you will need to know how to read the notes on the treble clef. To help you remember the letter names of the treble clef notes you might find it useful to think of a funny or memorable phrase. For example, notice how the notes on the lines of the treble clef stave (E, G, B, D, and F) can be used to spell out the phrase: **E**very **G**rizzly **B**ear **D**eserves **F**ood, and the notes in the spaces spell **FACE**. Feel free to experiment and make up your own phrase or rhyme if you find it easier to remember.

Letter names of notes on the lines of the treble clef:

E	G	B	D	F
Every	Grizzly	Bear	Deserves	Food

Letter names of notes in the spaces of the treble clef:

F	A	C	E

Notes of the bass clef

If you sing bass you will need to be able to read the letter names of the notes on the bass clef. At times, tenors find their line is written in the bass clef. If you are a treble, your voice will eventually change, and you might find yourself singing alto, tenor or bass one day – it is well worth seeing if you can remember these letter names now, and it will also come in handy if you decide to learn an instrument such as the piano which uses treble and bass clef, or another instrument written in the bass clef like the bassoon, cello or trombone.

Letter names of notes on the lines of the bass clef:

G	B	D	F	A
Good	Basses	Deserve	Food	Always

Letter names of notes in the spaces of the bass clef:

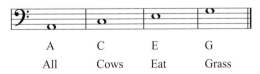

A	C	E	G
All	Cows	Eat	Grass

Note values

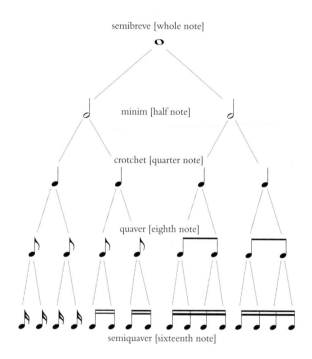

The note tree on the previous page shows the common note values. You may prefer to think of the note values in the following way:

o = A semibreve [whole note] lasts for 4 beats

♩ = A minim [half note] lasts for 2 beats

♩ = A crotchet [quarter note] lasts for 1 beat

♪ = A quaver [eighth note] lasts for ½ a beat

♪ = A semiquaver [sixteenth note] lasts for ¼ a beat

While the notes above are the most common, there are other notes that you will encounter during your singing. For example, the following note is known as a breve [double whole note]:

|o| = A breve [double whole note] lasts for 8 beats
(double the value of a semibreve)

Breves [double whole notes] are very rarely found in modern music but they were frequently used in early music. When singing from some older editions you may come across this note.

Dotted notes

A dot after a note makes it half as long again. For example:

♩. = ♩ + ♪   A dotted crotchet [dotted quarter note] lasts 1½ beats

♩. = ♩ + ♩   A dotted minim [dotted half note] lasts 3 beats

o· = o + ♩   A dotted semibreve [dotted whole note] lasts 6 beats

Ties

Two or more notes of the same pitch can be 'tied' together. This means that only the first note is sounded, the others are added on to the first note and held for their full value.

= 3 crotchet [quarter note] beats

= 5 crotchet [quarter note] beats

= 7 crotchet [quarter note] beats

Rests (silences)

Each note shape has a rest (silence) sign of exactly similar value:

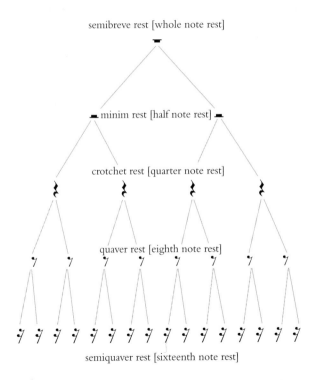

semibreve rest [whole note rest]

minim rest [half note rest]

crotchet rest [quarter note rest]

quaver rest [eighth note rest]

semiquaver rest [sixteenth note rest]

Time signatures

A time signature tells you how many beats or pulses there are in each bar. The top number tells you the number of beats in a bar. The bottom number tells you the type of beat in a bar.

For example:

2 - There are 2 beats in a bar
4 - The beats are crotchet [quarter note] beats

When looking at the bottom number of a time signature, you may find it helpful to refer to the note tree on page 55 to help you work out which note value is represented by which number. It is all worked out by how many beats fit into a semibreve [whole note].

For example:

There are 2 minims [half notes] in a semibreve [whole note]. Therefore, a minim [half note] beat is represented by the number '2' at the bottom of a key signature.

$\frac{3}{2}$ = 3 minim [half note] beats in a bar

There are 4 crotchets [quarter notes] in a semibreve [whole note]. Therefore, a crotchet [quarter note] beat is represented by the number '4' at the bottom of a key signature.

$\frac{3}{4}$ = 3 crotchet [quarter note] beats in a bar

Simple time signatures

Simple time signatures are any with a 2, 3 or 4 as the top number of the time signature. For example:

2	3	4		2	3	4		2	3	4
2	2	2		4	4	4		8	8	8

Compound time signatures

Compound time signatures are any where the top number can be divided by 3 (with the exception of 3 itself). For example:

6	9	12		6	9	12		6	9	12
2	2	2		4	4	4		8	8	8

Irregular time signatures

An irregular time signature is one where the bar (or top number of the time signature) cannot be divided into equal groups of 2 or 3 beats. For example:

5	7	11		5	7	11		5	7	11
2	2	2		4	4	4		8	8	8

Accidentals

The ♯, ♭ and ♮ signs that are found in a piece of music are called accidentals.

The ♯ sign raises the note that follows it by one semitone [half-step].

The ♭ sign lowers the note that follows it by one semitone [half-step].

The ♮ sign cancels any previous ♯ or ♭ signs, bringing the note back to its original pitch.

An accidental lasts until the end of the bar [measure]. For example:

1 is an F♯ because it is affected by the ♯ sign that appeared earlier in the same bar [measure].

2 is an F♮ because it is no longer affected by the ♯ sign that appeared in the previous bar [measure].

If you wanted to naturalise an accidental within the same bar [measure], a ♮ sign must be added:

Keys and scales

Each note in a scale has a technical name according to where it sits in the scale. This technical name is not the same as the pitch (or 'letter name') of the note. The pitch name is based on where the note sits on the stave. The technical name is based on the position of the note within the scale itself. In a scale of 8 notes, ascending, the technical names are listed below:

1st note	–	Tonic (Doh)
2nd note	–	Supertonic (Re)
3rd note	–	Mediant (Mi)
4th note	–	Subdominant (Fa)
5th note	–	Dominant (Soh)
6th note	–	Submediant (Lah)
7th note	–	Leading note (Ti)
8th note	–	Tonic (Doh)

Some singers find it easier to remember the position of the notes in the scale using the tonic sol-fa system – these are given in brackets alongside the technical note names for reference.

Not all pieces of music are written in the same key – that is, they do not all have the same note as their tonic or home note (Doh). However, a major scale (whatever key it is written in) always has the same pattern of notes – the distance (or interval) between each note of the scale is always the same. A major scale has the following pattern of tones (whole steps) and semitones (half steps):

If you started the scale on a note other than C, you would find that in order to keep the same pattern of tones and semitones, you would need to alter certain notes. For example, if you start on the note G, you would need to raise the seventh note to an F♯ in order to make sure that there was a whole tone between the sixth and seventh note, and a semitone between the seventh and eighth note:

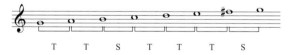

If you are singing a piece of music in the key of G, instead of seeing a ♯ sign in front of every note F in the piece, the sign is usually put at the beginning of the stave – this tells you that every F you see should be raised by a semitone and sung or played as an F♯. This is known as the key signature.

A complete list of key signatures is listed for your reference below:

The wheel of key signatures [Circle of fifths]

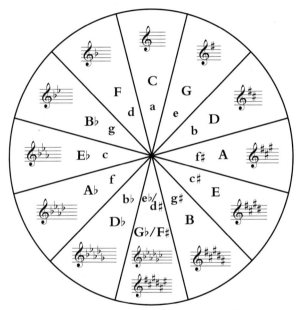

Major key signatures are in CAPITAL letters

Minor key signatures are in lower case letters

Musical terms and reference

In music many of the terms or instructions used are written in Italian. For your reference, here are some musical terms which are commonly used in church music. This is not an exhaustive list for all musical disciplines; if you encounter other terms not in this book you should refer to a music dictionary.

> Don't forget to refer to your Singer's Workbook for more help with dynamics, performance directions and how to pronounce these Italian words!

Terms referring to the dynamics (or volume) of the music:

Crescendo [***Cresc.***]	get gradually louder
Decrescendo [***Desc.***]	get gradually quieter
Diminuendo [***dim.***]	get gradually quieter
Fortissimo (or ***ff***)	very loudly
Forte (or ***f***)	loudly
Forte piano (or ***fp***)	loud, then immediately quiet
Forzando (or ***fz***)	forcing, accented
Mezzo forte (or ***mf***)	fairly loudly

Mezzo piano (or *mp*)   fairly quietly

Morendo   dying away

Niente   nothing (no sound)

Perdendosi   dying away

Piano (or *p*)   quietly

Pianissimo (or *pp*)   very quietly

Sforzando (or *sfz*)   sudden accent

Subito forte
(or *sub f*)   suddenly loud

Subito piano
(or *sub p*)   suddenly quiet

Pianissimo

Terms referring to the tempo (or speed) of the music:

A tempo	back to the previous speed
Accelerando (or *accel*)	getting gradually faster
Adagio	slowly
Allargando	broadening out, getting slower
Allegro	fast and lively
Allegretto	fairly fast
Andante	at a walking pace
Grave	slow and solemn
Larghetto	slow (but less slow than Largo)
Largo	slow and broad
Lento	very slowly
Moderato	at a moderate pace
Mosso	movement
Meno mosso	less movement
Piu mosso	more movement
Presto	very fast
Rallentando (or *rall.*)	getting gradually slower

Ritardando (or *rit.*)	getting gradually slower
Ritenuto	held back (get slower at once)
Rubato	with freedom of time (slowing and quickening freely)
Stringendo	getting faster
Tempo primo	back to the original speed
Vivace	lively, quick

Vivace

Terms referring to the character of the music:

Agitato	agitated
Animato	animated, lively
Appassionato	passionately
Cantabile	in a singing style
Con anima	with feeling, soul or spirit
Con brio	with vigour
Deciso	decisively
Delicato	delicately
Dolce	sweetly
Dolente	sad, mournful
Energico	energetically
Espressivo	with expression
Furioso	furious
Grandioso	grandly
Leggiero	lightly
Maestoso	majestically
Marcato	marked, accented
Pesante	heavy
Risoluto	bold, strong
Scherzo	a joke
Sonoro	resonant, with a rich tone

Sostenuto	sustained
Sotto voce	in an undertone
Tenuto	held on
Tranquillo	calmly
Triste	sad, sorrowful

Maestoso

Other general terms:

A cappella	without accompaniment
Accidentals	sharps, flats or natural signs written in the music but not already in the key signature
Ad libitum (or Ad lib.)	at will or as desired
Alla	in the style or manner of (e.g. 'Alla marcia' means in the style of a march)
Alto	the voice which lies in pitch below the Soprano or Treble but above the Tenor. When sung by an adult male it is often called 'Counter-tenor' or when sung by a female it is called 'Contralto'.
Anthem	a sacred choral composition, often with a biblical text, which may be with or without accompaniment
Antiphony, antiphonal singing	the alternate singing of two groups of voices, such as Decani and Cantoris, solo voice and chorus, or upper and lower voices

Assai   very

Baritone   a male voice which lies in pitch between the Tenor and the Bass

Bass   the lowest, or deepest male voice

Basso continuo   the continued bass; an instrumental bass part in early music, with figures (or numbers) under the bass notes to indicate the harmony that should be played on the keyboard instrument

Cantata   a composition in several movements, generally for soloists and chorus rather like a short oratorio

Cantor   a chanter. Someone who starts the singing, as in Plainsong, or who chants by him/herself as in the Litany, or helps animate the congregation to sing

Cantoris (or Can.)   in a cathedral, the side of the choir on which the Precentor (or Cantor) sits. Usually the left hand side on entering the choir from the nave

Chorale	a German hymn tune
Chord	two or more notes played or sung together
Chromatic	using all the semitones, as in the chromatic scale or in chromatic harmony
Clef	a sign used to determine the name and pitch of the notes on the stave. The treble clef and bass clef are most commonly used, but a C clef is sometimes used for alto and tenor parts.
Col, colla, con	with
Contralto	the female alto voice
Counter-tenor	the adult male alto voice
Da capo (or D.C.)	repeat from the beginning
Dal segno (or D.S.)	go back to the sign 𝄋
Decani (or Dec.)	in a cathedral, the side of the choir on which the Dean sits. Usually the right hand side on entering the choir from the nave.

Descant	an added part over the top of the melody, in hymns the descant is often sung by the trebles and sopranos while the other parts sing the melody in unison
Divisi (or div.)	divide into two or more groups
Extemporisation	the art of performing without preparation – of composing in the mind and playing the music on the spur of the moment. The same as improvisation.
Fauxbourdon or Faburden	an old term applied to certain types of harmony often involving the transfer of the melody from one voice part to another so that, for example, it may be sung by the tenors instead of the trebles
Fine	end
Fugue or Fuga	a composition in a strict style in which the tune (or subject) is first played or sung on its own, and then imitated, repeated or answered in each of the voice parts in turn

Harmony	the art of combining sounds to form chords and chordal progressions
Interval	the difference in pitch between two notes
Introit	a hymn or anthem sung at the start of a service, or while the priest enters the Sanctuary at Mass
Key-note	the tonic, or first note of the scale which gives its name to the key of a piece. Also known as 'Doh' in the sol-fa system.
Lay clerks (or Lay vicars)	the name given to the adult male singers in a Cathedral Choir
Lunga pausa	long pause
Ma non troppo	but not too much
Modulation	a change of key
Molto	much, very
Motet	a sacred composition such as an anthem for several voice parts. The words are usually taken from the Bible and are often in Latin.

Non	not
Opus	Latin for 'a work'. Many composers number or catalogue their compositions using Opus numbers e.g. 'Op. 1'.
Oratorio	a sacred drama based on a scriptural story and set to music for voices and instruments performed without the aid of scenery or action (e.g. Handel's *Messiah*).
Plainsong or Plainchant	an ancient chant or melody normally written on a stave of only four lines, in square or diamond shaped notes
Poco	a little
Poco a poco	little by little
Precentor	a member of the clergy, generally in a cathedral, responsible for the overall direction of the worship.
Prima, primo	first
Quasi	as if, almost
Quire	an old way of spelling 'choir'

Recitative	declamation in singing in which the note values are approximate and governed by the words (often found in Oratorio and Opera)
Secondam, second	second
Sempre	always
Senza	without
Simile	continue in the same way
Simplice	simple, simply
Sopra	above
Soprano	another name for Treble, and the name of the highest female voice
Sotto	below
Subito	suddenly
Staccato	short, detached notes
Stave or Staff	the five parallel lines on which music is written
Tacet	silent (often referring to a section of music, indicating that you should be silent during this section)

Tenor   the male voice pitched between the bass and the alto

Unison   'one sound' – in music this normally indicates that all the voices should sing the same melody together

Tutti   all, everybody

Verse   a portion of an anthem or service setting to be sung by one or more solo voices

Voce   voice

Voluntary   an organ piece played before or after a service. The word is derived from the fact that early voluntaries were often improvised.

THE MUSIC WE SING

There are many reasons why we choose to sing, and why we choose to join a choir. Some people want to feel more confident using their singing voice and feel happiest doing this within a 'group' situation rather than singing on their own. Others want to make new friends. Others want to contribute something to the life of their church. Whatever your reasons were for joining your choir, underpinning it all will be a love of singing and music.

This enjoyment of making music is absolutely vital when we sing in order to produce a performance with 'heart and soul' but as a singer you also have a job to do. Your job is to communicate the music and its meaning as best you can to those who are listening to you. This is quite a responsibility.

In order to be able to communicate effectively with your listeners you will need to understand:

The text

The music has been set to words (or lyrics) for a reason. Imagine that you are a story-teller, and you have an important story to tell every time you sing. You need to try and capture the imagination of the people who are listening to you. You will only be able to do this if you understand the meaning of the words yourself.

If the words are in a foreign language make sure you

find a translation (or ask your choir trainer or teacher to tell you what the words mean). Even if the words are in English, don't just sing them without thinking – what are they about? What mood, meaning or story are they trying to express? How can you put this across?

The music

If the words were the only important part of a song or anthem, you could just read them aloud like a poem or a Bible reading without any music at all. But the words have been set to music for a reason: to help you to express a particular mood or meaning.

Think of a text which has been set to music by more than one composer (e.g. 'The Lord is my shepherd' or 'Ave Maria') - although the words are the same, the music may make one version have a very different emotion or mood to another.

Every time you sing, think about the mood of the music as well as the meaning of the text. What mood is the music trying to convey? How can you put this across as effectively as possible in your performance?

The purpose of the piece

Very often a piece of music is written for a specific occasion or time of year. Rather than singing on 'automatic pilot' it is useful for you as a performer to know why a piece was written, and to think about why it is suitable for that theme, season, time of year or event.

As you progress as a singer you are likely to find yourself involved in concerts (choral and/or solo) and you may eventually become interested in running your own choir or teaching others to sing.

You will need to learn how to make suitable repertoire choices based on theme or season, perhaps choosing appropriate music for the time of year for your church choir, or building a themed concert/recital programme to perform as part of your music exams at school, or for solo performance purposes. Start thinking about how certain pieces of music fit with particular themes and/or times of the year now to build up a good store of knowledge!

There are lots of other interesting bits of information you can find out about the music you sing and you will be asked to research some of this if you are taking part in the *Voice for Life* training scheme. If you want to know more about the music you sing have a look in your Singer's Workbook for some ideas on how to find out more, and what questions you could consider.

Here are the basic questions a singer should ask themselves every time they sing:

+ What are the words about? What mood, meaning or story are they trying to express?

+ Are there any words I don't understand?

+ Are there any words I don't know how to pronounce? (If so, ask for help!)

+ What is the mood of the music?

+ How does the music help me put across the meaning of the words?

+ Is this piece suitable for a particular time of year/season or theme?

+ Most importantly: am I really communicating all this to my listeners through my performance?

Remember: it is important as a singer that you don't just perform on 'automatic pilot'. Make sure you know *why* you are singing what you are singing, and *what* you are singing about.

BELONGING TO THE CHOIR

Your choir is a team. In a sports team all the members of the team must participate fully for the team to function at its best. If some members of the team do not participate then the other members become tired more quickly and cannot compete against a team where all the members are fully involved. This is the same as a choir. Your choir will function at its best when every member of the choir participates fully – singing to the best of their ability, and being as cooperative and helpful to the choir trainer as possible.

Whoever you are:

- a new member of the choir who does not yet know all the choir's routines and duties

- a beginner singer who does not feel very confident with their singing voice

- someone who is quite shy and does not know very many people in the choir

- an extremely confident and experienced singer who has been in the choir for a long time

remember that every singer in the choir matters! You matter. Whether you feel that you are a confident singer or not, your commitment is vital in order for your choir to function at its best. Aim to show your commitment in the following ways:

Be the best singer & musician you can

It is important that you constantly work on improving both your singing voice and your musical ability. The more each individual voice improves, the better and stronger the overall sound of the choir will be. The more each singer improves at music-reading, the faster the choir will be able to learn new music.

Always contribute to the overall sound

Whether you feel confident with your voice or not, every singer should make sure they participate fully during rehearsals and services/performances. Don't assume that no one will notice if you don't sing, and make sure you don't 'switch off'. Always aim to stay focused and give your best.

Be reliable

Be on time for rehearsals and services. Ideally you should arrive slightly before the start time so you are ready to begin on time, and make sure you have the necessary equipment with you (e.g. pencil, music, *Voice for Life* Singer's Workbook, etc). Aim for the best attendance record you can. When you cannot attend a rehearsal or service/performance always remember to tell your choir trainer or teacher in advance so they can plan accordingly.

Be co-operative & helpful

Make sure you listen and respond well in rehearsals and services to what you are being asked to do (e.g. quickly finding the right music, page or bar as directed by your trainer). If you notice other less experienced members of the choir are struggling, helping them quietly and without creating a fuss will be much appreciated by the singer and your choir trainer. Whether you have been in the choir for a long time, or are a new member, always set an example to others in the choir through your singing and your behaviour.

Make sure everyone in the choir feels welcome and part of the team

Do you remember what it was like when you first joined the choir? Did you know anyone in the choir already? Perhaps someone befriended you and helped you to know what you needed to do like where to sit, and where to find your music. Even for long standing members of a choir, it makes attending rehearsals much more enjoyable if the other singers are friendly and welcoming. Always try to be aware of the other singers in your choir, making sure they feel 'included'. In particular, keep an eye out for singers who are new or a bit shy – if you make them feel welcome and an important part of the team, they are more likely to enjoy their time in the choir. This will all help the team to function at its best.

If you think someone in the choir is being treated unfairly, hurt or bullied (perhaps they are being called names or teased), or if this is happening to you, then you need to tell someone what is going on, so the situation can be dealt with. Tell the choir trainer and/ or your parents or guardian. If you find that hard to do in person, you could write a note explaining how you feel. But if you need further help and advice on being bullied, visit: www.bullying.co.uk.

Finally, be aware that your choir trainer or teacher will be working very hard to run the choir and there are lots of aspects of organisation that go on behind the scenes to make everything work smoothly. Try using your initiative to look for ways to help make your choir trainer's job easier (e.g. you could offer to collect up the music at the end of a rehearsal, or put the chairs away).

> Remember: Every singer in your choir is an important and valuable member of the team. When every singer is 100% committed, the choir can function to the best of its ability.

Hints and tips for Head Choristers

If you are reading this section, you have probably been appointed as Head Chorister of your choir – congratulations! Just as a sports team needs a captain, so a choir needs a Head Chorister. You have an important job to do and carry a great responsibility in three main areas:

+ Your influence and example will be felt throughout the choir. You are there to set an example from the top. Other singers will take their lead from you musically, but they will also be influenced by your attitude, behaviour and general organisation.

+ Less experienced singers need your help, encouragement and leadership in order to find their place in the choir and to progress.

+ Your choir trainer will be relying on you. An orchestra has a leader upon whom the conductor depends. In the same way, you are the musical leader of your choir. You must keep your vocal line secure and aim for the highest possible musical standards at all times.

You will need to discuss with your choir trainer or teacher your exact duties as a Head Chorister. This differs from choir to choir depending on whether you are part of a church choir, a school choir or community choir. However, here are some hints and tips to help you in your role:

+ Only ask others to do what you would be prepared to do yourself.

+ Be fair. Never show favouritism.

+ Make sure you are clear when you ask others to do something. Don't assume they know what to do.

+ Always give praise and encouragement when your singers have done well. This shows that you notice them and appreciate their efforts.

+ You are most likely to influence others by your example rather than by what you say. If you sing well and concentrate during rehearsals and performances then others are more likely to imitate this behaviour. If you talk during rehearsals or sing badly, do not be surprised when others do the same.

+ Do not interfere with your choir trainer's instructions and never fuss during a rehearsal.

+ When you need to give orders to other singers (or to your Team Leaders if your choir has them), do this in a quiet, confident and persuasive way. Never shout and try not to be bossy.

+ Do not bully other singers and do not tolerate any bullying among your singers.

+ Look ahead: see what needs to be done before you are asked by the choir trainer, and ensure it is done quietly and efficiently either by you or someone else.

Remember: Lead by example.

Good luck in your new role as Head Chorister of your choir!

THE CHORISTER'S PRAYER

> Bless, O Lord, us thy servants,
> who minister in thy temple.
> Grant that what we sing with our lips,
> we may believe in our hearts,
> and what we believe in our hearts,
> we may show forth in our lives.
> Through Jesus Christ our Lord.
> Amen.

The *Chorister's Prayer* seems to have first appeared in the *Choirboy's Pocket Book*, published by the *School of English Church Music* (the former name of the RSCM) in 1934. Despite being so well known, the prayer is not given an author in this source (some say it was the RSCM's founder, Sir Sydney Nicholson, while others link it to Cosmo Gordon Lang, who became Archbishop of Canterbury in 1929).

The English version of this Prayer appears to be very close to the Latin in the Pontificale Romanum of 1595–6 in the form for admitting a Psalmista or Cantor:

Vide, ut, quod ore cantas, corde credas, et quod core credis, operibus comprobes.

It may be even older (perhaps 13th or 14th century).

THE CHURCH AND ITS WORSHIP

by Peter Moger

The Church's Calendar

As each new year comes around, there are always special dates to mark on the calendar. Every year we celebrate our own birthday, and those of members of our family and our friends. Other events, too, always happen at the same time each year: a new school year always begins in September, and the FA Cup Final is usually held in mid-May. The dates in the calendar and the changing of the seasons help give shape to our lives from year to year. It's the same in the Church, which also organises each year by a special calendar.

Two types of time

The Christian Year is divided into two types of time: *seasonal time* and *ordinary time*. About half the year falls in seasonal time, and half in ordinary time.

Seasonal time covers those parts of the year when we are celebrating something special to do with the Christian faith. Within seasonal time there are two blocks or cycles: the *Christmas cycle* and the *Easter (or Paschal) cycle*.

The Christmas cycle:

Advent – Christmas - Epiphany

The Christmas cycle (and the Church's new year) begins four Sundays before Christmas Day with the season of **Advent**. Advent (which means 'coming' or 'arrival') is a time of waiting and preparation, both for Christmas itself, and for the time when Jesus will finally return in glory (sometimes called the 'Second Coming'). The idea of opening windows on an Advent Calendar, or lighting an Advent Candle helps us count down the days of the season to Christmas Day.

On **Christmas** Day (25 December) we celebrate the birth of Jesus (*Luke* 2: 1–7), through which God shares our life by being born as a human being. This leads, 12 days later (6 January) into the **Epiphany** season. Epiphany means 'showing' or 'manifestation', so throughout this season we focus on who Jesus is and what he did when he was on earth. The Epiphany season focuses on three important events: the visit of the Wise Men to the child Jesus (*Matthew* 2: 1–12), the baptism of Jesus by John in the River Jordan (*Matthew* 3: 13–17), and Jesus' first miracle – the turning of water into wine at a wedding at Cana (*John* 2: 1–11). The Christmas cycle ends 40 days after Christmas Day with the Feast of the Presentation of Christ in the Temple – often called **Candlemas** – (*Luke* 2: 22–40) on 2 February.

The Easter cycle:

Lent – Passiontide – Eastertide

The Easter cycle begins 6 ½ weeks before Easter Day on Ash Wednesday with the season of **Lent**. Lent lasts for 40 days, reminding us of the 40 days and nights Jesus spent in the wilderness (*Matthew 4: 1–11*). The first Christians used Lent to prepare for their baptism, and Christians today still use this time to draw closer to God. To help them do this, some people give up luxuries during Lent, take on extra study or prayer, or commit to doing things to help others.

 For some good ideas for things to do in Lent, have a look at www.livelent.net

The last part of Lent is sometimes called **Passiontide**, a name which comes from the Latin word *passio*, meaning 'I suffer'. This is the season when we think about Jesus' death for us on the cross.

The week before Easter is **Holy Week** – the most important week of the Christian Year. In Holy Week, the Church commemorates in its worship the events that happened leading up to the death and resurrection of Jesus.

Holy Week begins with **Palm Sunday**, when we recall Jesus being welcomed by the crowds as he rode into Jerusalem (*Mark 11: 1–10*). The Thursday of Holy Week is called **Maundy Thursday** (from the Latin word *mandatum*, meaning 'commandment'). On this day we remember Jesus' Last Supper with his disciples. It was at this meal that Jesus washed his disciples' feet (*John 13: 1–11*) and gave them two commandments: to 'love one another' (*John 13: 14*) and to take and share bread and wine in remembrance of him (*Luke 22: 19–20*).

The Friday of Holy Week, **Good Friday**, recalls the day when Jesus died on the Cross (*John 19: 16–37*). This is often celebrated by services including a long reading of the story of Jesus' death from the Gospels, prayer and carrying a large cross, possibly in church, or perhaps in the open air.

The day before Easter Day (sometimes called **Holy Saturday** or **Easter Eve**) is a quiet day as we remember Jesus' body lying in the tomb.

Easter Day is the most joyful day of the Christian Year: the day when we celebrate Jesus' rising from the dead (*John 20: 1–10*) and the truth that he is alive today. Some Easter services begin before dawn and include the lighting of an Easter (or 'Paschal') candle to remind us that Jesus, the Light of the World, is risen from death. Most churches have special services on this day.

The Easter season (or 'Eastertide') lasts for 50 days after Easter Day. During this time we continue to think about Jesus being alive – and how that affects us today.

Ascension Day (always on a Thursday, 40 days after Easter) is a celebration of Jesus' return to heaven (*Luke 24: 50–53*) and his promise that he will always be with us (*Matthew 28: 20b*).

The season ends 10 days later on the Day of **Pentecost** (Whit Sunday), when we celebrate the gift of God's Holy Spirit (*Acts 2: 1–21*). The Holy Spirit lives in all Christians and gives life to God's people.

Ordinary time

In seasonal time, the Church's worship tends to have a clear focus or theme. But for the rest of the year, the Church keeps 'ordinary time'. It's as though we need some time simply to get on with everyday 'ordinary' life as Christians!

There are two periods of Ordinary Time. The first – from 3 February to Ash Wednesday – is quite short, and can be very short indeed if Easter is early. The second is much longer, and runs from the day after Pentecost to the day before Advent Sunday. The first Sunday in this period of Ordinary Time is **Trinity Sunday** – the day we celebrate that God is Father, Son and Holy Spirit. The Sundays during this long period of Ordinary Time are called the 'Sundays after Trinity.' The last weeks of the Christian year are marked by 'Sundays before Advent' and include celebrations of the saints (**All Saints' Day**), those who have died (**All Souls' Day**) and **Remembrance Sunday**.

Colours

In many churches, colours are used to mark the seasons of the Christian Year.

White (or gold) is used for times of big celebration: Christmas, Epiphany, Easter and some saints' days.

Red is the colour of fire and so is used to celebrate the coming of the Holy Spirit at Pentecost. It's also the colour of blood, and so it's used in Passiontide, and to celebrate those Christians who have died for their faith (martyrs).

Purple is a colour sometimes linked with suffering, and is used during the seasons of Lent and Advent.

At all other times (in Ordinary Time), **Green** is used.

Green is the colour of growth and of life: it reminds us that, as Christians, we must always be growing into the people God has made us to be.

The Christian Year

SEASON	DATES	THEMES	COLOUR
Advent	4 Sundays before Christmas	Waiting, The promise of light in darkness, Preparation for Jesus' coming at Christmas & his second coming at the end of time	Purple
Christmas	25 December to 5 January	The birth of Jesus (God born as a human being)	White/Gold
Epiphany	6 January to 2 February Candlemas	The visit of the Wise Men to Jesus	White/Gold
Ordinary Time	3 February to Shrove Tuesday	[Sometimes a very short season] Growth (Creation)	Green
Lent	Ash Wednesday to fifth Sunday of Lent	Asking God's forgiveness, self-denial, Preparing for Easter (orginally linked with Baptism)	Purple

Passiontide (Holy Week)	5 Sunday of Lent to Easter Eve	Jesus' death for us on the Cross	Purple/ Red
Eastertide	Easter Day to Ascension Day (40 days)	Jesus' rising from the dead, Resurrection hope for us all, Living in the light of the Resurrection	White/ Gold
Ascensiontide	Ascension Day to Pentecost (10 days)	Praying for the gift of the Holy Spirit	White/ Gold
Ordinary Time ('Sundays after Trinity')	Day after Pentecost to 31 October	Growth in faith Christian living Continuous reading of the scriptures	Green (White for Trinity Sunday)
(Sundays before Advent)	1 November (All Saints Day) to Eve of Advent Sunday	The Kingdom of God, The Departed (All Saints and All Souls), Remembrance, Christ the King (Sunday before Advent)	Red (or Green)

Other special days

Some branches of the Church keep other special days throughout the year. Roman Catholics and Anglicans celebrate saints' days and some other important holy days. The main celebrations are:

January 1	The Naming and Circumcision of Jesus (C of E)
	Mary, Mother of God (RC)
January 25	The Conversion of Paul (an enemy of Christians who converted when he met the risen Jesus on the road to Damascus)
February 2	The Presentation of Jesus in the Temple (Candlemas)
March 19	Joseph of Nazareth, Husband of the Blessed Virgin Mary
March 25	The Annunciation of Our Lord to the Blessed Virgin Mary
April 23	George, Martyr, Patron Saint of England
April 25	Mark the Evangelist (writer of the Gospel)
May 1	Philip and James, Apostles

May 14	Matthias the Apostle (took the place of Judas Iscariot, who betrayed Jesus)
May 31	The Visit of the Blessed Virgin Mary to Elizabeth
June 11	Barnabas the Apostle (Missionary and companion of Paul)
June 24	The Birth of John the Baptist (John prepared the way for Jesus by preaching and baptizing)
June 29	Peter the Apostle (his name means 'rock' – he was the 'foundation stone' of the Church)
July 3	Thomas the Apostle (Thomas doubted Jesus had risen from the dead until he had seen him)
July 22	Mary Magdalen (the first person to see Jesus risen from the dead)
July 25	James the Apostle (brother of St John, killed for his faith by King Herod)
August 6	The Transfiguration of Our Lord
August 15	The Blessed Virgin Mary
August 24	Bartholomew the Apostle
September 14	Holy Cross Day

September 21	Matthew, Apostle & Evangelist (Gospel-writer)
September 29	Michael and All Angels
October 18	Luke, Evangelist (writer of a Gospel and the Acts of the Apostles)
October 28	Simon and Jude, Apostles
November 1	All Saints' Day
November 2	Commemoration of the Faithful Departed (All Souls)
November 30	Andrew the Apostle
December 26	Stephen, Deacon (the first person to be killed for being a Christian)
December 27	John, Apostle & Evangelist (writer of a Gospel, three letters and Revelation)
December 28	The Holy Innocents (the children killed by King Herod)
Thursday after Trinity Sunday	Corpus Christi (Thanksgiving for Holy Communion)
Sunday before Advent	Feast of Christ the King

Methodists celebrate Wesley Day (24 May) as the day of the conversion of John Wesley.

A number of Free Churches celebrate Church Anniversaries – the date of the founding of their local church.

A GUIDE TO CHURCH SERVICES

Worship

The word worship comes from an old English word *weorthschipe* meaning 'to give worth or value to someone or something'. To worship as a Christian means to give God the glory, worth and honour that is his by right. People have always worshipped. It's as though, deep within all human beings is the instinct to worship something or someone.

The Bible shows us that, as people became more aware of God, so their worship developed. By the time of King David, worship was highly organised, and involved music. You can read about this in *1 Chronicles 15*. After the death and resurrection of Jesus, the first Christians began to develop their own patterns of worship. They chose Sunday as the main day of celebration, because that was the day on which Jesus rose from the dead.

Christian worship is something God's people do together. Our own personal Christian faith is really important, but we are also part of something much bigger – the Christian Church. In the Bible, St Paul reminds us that the Church is rather like a body, with lots of different parts, each with their own jobs to do (*1 Corinthians 12:12–31*). None of us can work properly without the other parts of the body. It's important to worship God and serve him together.

But worship is not just something we do in church and on Sundays. It's about the whole of our life: we show our love for God and our worship of him by the way we live. To be real worshippers, we must open ourselves to God's love and trust him in every part of our lives. We can then become more fully the people God wants us to be. Worship will then be more about who we are than about what we do.

Today there are many branches of the Christian Church, each with its own traditions and styles of worship. Most churches have recognised 'services' which they hold regularly.

There are two services, though, which are common to almost all Christians. These are the sacraments of Baptism and Holy Communion. Both were commanded by Jesus himself. St Matthew records Jesus saying 'Go and make disciples of all nations, baptizing them in the name of the Father, and of the Son and of the Holy Spirit (*Matthew 28: 19*). And so Baptism, whether for a baby whose parents promise to bring him / her up as a Christian, or for an adult who has come to faith, is the sign of the new life God offers us in Jesus, and of entry into the Christian Church.

For those of us who sing in choirs, it's always helpful to remember that when we worship, we do it first of all for God. We also help lead the worship of the congregation, of course, but our worship is offered whether or not there happens to be a congregation. For choristers who sing in cathedrals, it can sometimes seem strange to be singing Evensong with a choir of twenty-five, three or four ministers and just two or three in the congregation on a dark February evening! It is on occasions like this that we are reminded most of all that the worship we offer is for God, and that as we worship, we join our prayers and praises with those who worship at all times around his throne in heaven.

Holy Communion

When Jesus shared his last meal with his friends (the Last Supper), he took bread and wine and said 'This is my body... this is my blood ... do this in remembrance of me' (*Luke 22: 19–20*).

Christians have been doing just that for almost 2000 years! The service is called by several names: Holy Communion, the Eucharist, the Mass, the Lord's Supper – but all involve taking bread and wine in remembrance of Jesus.

A Holy Communion service (Eucharist) has four sections:

The Gathering

The Liturgy of the Word

The Liturgy of the Sacrament

The Dismissal

The Gathering

We come together as God's people

- The priest greets the people

- A prayer may be said together

- A hymn or song may be sung

We ask God to forgive the things in our lives which are wrong

- We confess our sins

- Sometimes this includes the singing of the **Kyrie**, a prayer for mercy

- The priest tells us that God forgives us

We praise God

- Usually by singing the **Gloria in excelsis** (*Glory to God in the highest*)

We pray a Collect

- Everyone prays silently

- The priest then 'collects' everyone's prayers together in a special prayer for the day

The Liturgy of the Word

We hear the Bible read

+ There may be readings from the Old Testament and New Testament

+ A Psalm, hymn or songs may be sung

+ There is always a reading from one of the Gospels

A sermon or talk follows the readings

+ This tries to help us understand God's word in the Bible and apply it to our lives as Christians today

We often affirm our faith in God by saying or singing a **Creed** (*Credo*) together

We pray Prayers of Intercession. In these, we pray for:

+ the world

+ the Church

+ our local community

+ those in special need

+ those who have died

The Liturgy of the Sacrament

We share the Peace

- This reminds us that we need to be on good terms with one another before we come to Communion

Bread and wine are placed on the Holy Table

- We often sing a hymn while this happens

The priest prays the Eucharistic Prayer. In this,

- we thank God for his love shown to us in Jesus

- we sing words – the **Sanctus** and **Benedictus** – which help us remember that we are joining our worship on earth with the worship of the saints and angels in heaven

- we remember Jesus' death on the cross

- we recall his command to take and share bread and wine

- we pray that, through the Holy Spirit, the bread and wine would be Jesus' body and blood for us

We pray the Lord's Prayer together

The bread is broken

+ While this happens, we might say or sing the **Agnus Dei**, a prayer to Jesus for mercy and peace

We receive the broken bread and the wine

The Dismissal

We receive God's blessing

We are sent out – with a job to do: to take God's love and the message of Jesus to those we meet in daily life.

Christians vary in their views about who may receive Holy Communion. In the Orthodox Church, Communion is given to all baptized worshippers (including babies!). In the Roman Catholic Church, baptized children are admitted to Communion by the parish priest. In the Church of England, Communion is given only after a baptized person has been either confirmed by the bishop or – if the parish and bishop agree – admitted to Holy Communion by the local priest. Admission of baptized children to Communion takes place after a teaching course in the local church.

Services of the Word

Not all Church services are services of Holy Communion. Sometimes, God's people meet simply to praise, to pray and to hear his word. Because the Bible tends to be the main focus of these services, they are sometimes called 'Services of the Word'.

These also tend to be in four main sections:

A Gathering

+ This will usually include some praise & confession of sin

+ It might include some Responses sung by the minister and the choir or congregation

A section based around The Word of God

+ The Bible is read

+ Psalms, Canticles or songs may be sung

+ A sermon or talk may be given

Prayer

+ We pray for the world, the Church and people in need

Dismissal

+ We are sent with God's blessing to live as his people in the world

Two common Services of the Word in the Church of England are **Morning Prayer** (often called **Matins**) and **Evening Prayer** (often called **Evensong**). These services were devised by Archbishop Thomas Cranmer in the 16th century and were included in the first ever service book in English, the Book of Common Prayer (1549). Today, we celebrate Morning and Evening Prayer either in the traditional version from the 1662 Book of Common Prayer or in the modern version from Common Worship (2000).

Morning and Evening Prayer follow this structure:

An **Introduction** in which we prepare to meet with God by

+ confessing our sins

+ praising God (in both Morning and Evening Prayer, the minister and congregation / choir sing or say a set of Versicles and Responses) and in Morning Prayer, this is followed by the canticle known as the Venite (Psalm 95).

A long, central section based around **The Word of God**:

+ Psalms

+ A reading from the Old Testament

+ A canticle (in the Book of Common Prayer, this is the *Te Deum* or the *Benedicite* in the morning, and the *Magnificat* in the evening)

+ A reading from the New Testament

+ A canticle (in the book of Common Prayer,
  this is the *Benedictus* or *Jubilate Deo*
  in the morning, and the *Nunc Dimittis* in
  the evening)

+ The Apostles' Creed

A short collection of **Prayers**:

+ These include the *Lesser Litany*, the *Lord's
  Prayer*, another set of *Versicles and Responses* and
  three Collects.

An **Anthem** (sung by the choir, if there is one)

Some concluding prayers, ending with the words of
The Grace.

Usually, hymns, a sermon and further prayers are
added to this structure.

In different branches of the Church, Services of the Word have other names. Here are some of them:

- ✦ Morning Worship

- ✦ Morning (or Evening) Service

- ✦ Family Service

- ✦ Vespers

- ✦ Compline (sometimes called 'Night Prayer')

- ✦ Prayer and Praise

- ✦ Parish Praise

Does your church have a 'service of the word' with a different name?

Songs from the Bible

In *Services of the Word* (especially Morning and Evening Prayer), the Bible readings are often followed by a Canticle. This is a set of words (usually) from the Bible, designed to be sung in worship. Examples of Canticles which are often sung are:

+ **Magnificat**, the song Mary sang after hearing the news that she was going to give birth to God's Son. It is taken from *Luke 1: 46–55*

+ **Benedictus**, the song sung by Zechariah after the birth of his son, John the Baptist. It can be found in *Luke 1: 68–79*

+ **Nunc Dimittis**, the song of Simeon, sung after he recognized Jesus as the Saviour of all people. Found in *Luke 2: 29–32*

+ **Jubilate Deo** – Psalm 100, a song which invites us to praise God.

+ **Venite** – Psalm 95, a song which invites us to praise God.

+ **Benedicite**, a song of creation's praise to God, taken from the Song of the Three in the Apocrypha.

+ **Te Deum Laudamus**, a hymn beginning 'We praise thee O God' which is not in the Bible but is one of the songs of the early Church.

Other parts of the Bible are also sometimes sung as canticles. These include several passages which were probably sung in the first centuries of the Christian Church and which the writers of the New Testament included in their books, e.g. **The Song of Christ's Glory** (*Philippians 2: 5–11*), **Great and Wonderful** (*Revelation 15: 3–4*), and also some important passages from the Old Testament, e.g. **The Song of Moses and Miriam** (*Exodus 15*).

Canticles are sometimes sung by the choir in a specially composed setting. A composer will sometimes set all the canticles for Morning or Evening Prayer, often in the same key. So 'Stanford in A' refers to Stanford's canticle settings in A major for Morning and Evening Prayer.

Other special services

As well as the regular services of Holy Communion and Services of the Word, most churches hold special services called Pastoral Services. These help mark important moments in human life and include:

+ Thanksgiving for the Gift of a Child

+ Baptism

+ Marriage

+ Re-affirmation of Marriage Vows

+ Funerals

+ Memorial Services

These services all have the same shape as a Service of the Word, and may sometimes be combined with a service of Holy Communion.

Most churches also hold a number of services each year which reflect the church's links with the local community. In the Church of England and the Roman Catholic Church, many churches are 'parish churches' and serve a local area such as a village, town, or part of a town or city. This link is a really important part of what it means to be the Church. As William Temple, a famous Archbishop of Canterbury, once said, 'The Church is the only institution which exists for the benefit of non-members.'

Services which link with the local community might include a service for Remembrance Sunday, a Civic Service (where prayer is offered for the Town/Parish Council and the Mayor), or services for local hospitals, schools or uniformed organisations (e.g. Scouts, Guides, Air Cadets etc). These services will often involve a number of local churches working together.

Different forms of worship

The worship in some churches follows a written order (sometimes called a 'liturgy'), while in others, it tends to take freer forms. Some churches have a mixture of fixed and free forms of worship.

The Church of England has two sets of liturgy. The first is the Book of Common Prayer which was first written in 1549. The version we have now dates from 1662. It contains services of great beauty, written in the English language of the 16th and 17th centuries. Many churches continue to use the Book of Common Prayer for at least some of their worship, particularly those churches which sing Evensong.

The second set of liturgy in the Church of England is Common Worship. This was produced between 2000 and 2008 and includes a large number of services, prayers and instructions to help local churches plan and conduct their worship. There are services of Holy Communion, services of the word, baptism and confirmation services, marriage and funeral services, healing and ordination services and a large number of services for special occasions in the Christian Year. Most of Common Worship is in modern language, and many of the shapes and some of the words found here are the same as those in the worship books of the Roman Catholic, Methodist and Lutheran Churches.

SOME DIFFICULT WORDS USED IN WORSHIP

Absolution   Words spoken by a priest declaring God's forgiveness after the people have confessed their sin.

Agnus Dei   The words (Latin) mean 'Lamb of God'. The Agnus Dei is a prayer to Jesus who 'takes away the sin of the world' to 'have mercy on us' and 'grant us peace'. It is sung as the bread at Holy Communion is broken.

Altar   The altar (sometimes called the Holy Table or Communion Table) is the table on which the bread and wine at Communion are placed.

Anthem   A piece of music sung by the choir during worship.

Apostolic   A word used to describe the Church because it follows the teaching of the Apostles.

Benedictus
A Latin word meaning 'Blessed'. There are two different sets of words with this name. One is a Canticle, often sung at Morning Prayer. The other is a verse from Psalm *118* which often follows the Sanctus in the Eucharistic Prayer.

Canticle
A Canticle is a collection of words (usually) from the Bible which are designed to be sung in worship. Examples of Canticles are the Magnificat (which comes from *Luke 1: 46–55*), the Benedictus (*Luke 1: 68–79*) and Nunc Dimittis (*Luke 2: 29–32*).

Catholic
A word meaning 'universal', used to describe the world-wide Church.

Collect
A collect is a prayer which 'collects together' the prayers of everyone. In most churches, this happens in the Gathering. At Matins and Evensong, three collects are said or sung towards the end of the service.

Compline
A late evening service, sometimes called *'Night Prayer'*.

Confession   It's hard to live as Christians and we often get it wrong. Because of this, most services include a 'confession' in which we ask God to forgive us our sins: the wrong things we have said, thought or done. In some churches there is also a tradition of making a private confession to a priest.

Creed   A Creed is a statement of what we believe. Christians have traditionally used two Creeds in worship: the Nicene Creed (at Holy Communion) and the Apostles' Creed (at Morning and Evening Prayer), but some churches also have other authorised Affirmations of Faith, most of which are taken from the Bible. If parts of the service are sung in Latin, the Creed will be called the Credo.

Deacon   In the Roman Catholic Church and Church of England, a Deacon is an ordained minister who assists a priest with whom he or she works.

Epistle

An epistle is a letter. The Bible contains several epistles, written by important early Christian leaders (like Peter, Paul and John) to newly-formed churches in the decades after Jesus' resurrection. A Communion service often includes a reading from an epistle.

Eucharist

(see Holy Communion)

Eucharistic Prayer

The prayer prayed over the bread and wine at Holy Communion.

Evensong

Another name for Evening Prayer.

Font

The font is a large bowl (often made of stone) in which Christians are baptised. The traditional place for a font is by the church door – because baptism marks the beginning of our life as a Christian. Have you seen the font where you were baptised?

Gloria

A Latin word meaning 'Glory'. There are two different Glorias often sung in worship. One is the Gloria in excelsis, an ancient hymn beginning 'Glory to God in the highest...' which forms part of the Holy Communion service. The other is the Gloria Patri. It begins 'Glory [be] to the Father, and to the Son and to the Holy Spirit / Ghost...' and is usually sung after a Psalm or Canticle.

Gospel

The word 'Gospel' means 'good news'. Four of the books of the Bible are Gospels (Matthew, Mark, Luke and John). These books record the story of Jesus: his birth and life – what he did and said. There is always a reading from one of the Gospels at a Holy Communion Service. In most churches, the congregation stands to hear this Gospel reading: it is as though, when we hear the words of Jesus in the Gospel, we come face-to-face with Jesus himself.

Gradual   A hymn or psalm sung before the reading of the Gospel at Holy Communion.

Incarnate   The word used to describe how God became a human being and lived on earth in the person of Jesus.

Intercession   This is prayer which is offered on behalf of someone else. Christian worship has always included prayer of intercession: for the Church, for the world and for those in need.

Kyrie   This word is Greek for 'Lord' and is the first word of a prayer often said or sung towards the beginning of a Communion Service (Eucharist). The prayer is very simple: 'Kyrie eleison, Christe eleison, Kyrie eleison' 'Lord, have mercy; Christ, have mercy; Lord, have mercy.'

Lord's Prayer   When Jesus' disciples asked him to teach them to pray, he gave them this pattern (see *Matthew 6: 9–15*.) All Christians pray this prayer, though churches sometimes use slightly different versions.

Magnificat   The song Mary sang after hearing the news that she was going to give birth to God's Son. It is taken from *Luke 1: 46–55*

Matins   Another name for Morning Prayer.

New Testament   The New Testament contains the last 27 books of the Bible and was written shortly after the time of Jesus. It includes the accounts of Jesus' life and the early Church.

Nunc Dimittis   The song of Simeon, sung after he recognized Jesus as the Saviour of all people. Found in *Luke 2: 29–32*

Offertory   Strangely, this has nothing to do with money! The Offertory is the presentation of the bread and wine for Communion at the altar. The collection of money during the service is an Offering!

Old Testament   The Old Testament contains the first 39 books of the Bible and dates from before the time of Jesus.

Prayer of Humble Access

A prayer written by Archbishop Thomas Cranmer for the first Book of Common Prayer, to be said just before receiving Communion. It asks that, through receiving the bread and wine, we may 'live in [Christ] and he in us.'

Psalm

The Psalms are the songs of God's people from the Old Testament. There are 150 of them and they have a special place in both Jewish and Christian worship. Which is the longest Psalm? And which is the shortest?

Psalter

A book containing the Psalms. In churches where Psalms are sung, the Psalms are often printed with music, and 'pointed', to show how the words fit the music.

Reader

In the Church of England, a licensed Reader is a lay minister: someone who is not ordained but trained and licensed to lead certain forms of worship. In the Methodist Church, lay ministers are called Local Preachers.

Sacrament   A gift of God in which people
receive something they cannot
see in the shape of something
ordinary and visible which
they can see. e.g. In Holy
Communion, we receive the
body and blood of Christ in the
form of bread and wine. Jesus
left us 2 sacraments: Baptism
and Holy Communion. Some
branches of the Church accept 5
more sacraments: Confirmation,
Anointing (sometimes called
'Unction'), Penance, Ordination
and Marriage.

Saint's Day   A day in the Church's Calendar to
celebrate a holy man or woman.

Sanctus   A Latin word meaning 'Holy'.
The Sanctus forms part of the
Communion service, where
it is said or sung as part of the
Eucharistic Prayer. The words are
found in the Bible (*Isaiah 6: 3*) and
Revelation 4: 8).

Sursum Corda   The Latin words meaning 'Lift up your hearts' – words spoken or sung by the priest and people at the start of the Eucharistic Prayer.

Versicles and Responses   A set of sentences (often taken from the Bible) which are sung or said by a minister and choir / congregation. The minister sings the versicle, and the choir replies with the response.

Voluntary   A piece of music played on the organ before, during or after a service.

WHAT WE WEAR IN CHURCH

Different churches have different traditions of what the ministers might be expected to wear in worship. In many (but not all) churches, the ministers wear special robes to lead worship.

Cassock   This is the basic garment worn by ministers (often black) and choir members (often coloured).

Surplice   This is a loose white garment with wide sleeves worn over the cassock by some choirs, and by lay and ordained ministers at certain services.

Scarf

At a Service of the Word (see above), the minister might wear a scarf (sometimes called a 'preaching scarf') over his/her surplice. A scarf is blue for a lay minister (Reader) and black for a deacon or priest.

Hood

At some services (usually Morning or Evening Prayer), an academic hood may be worn by the minister or by members of the choir. Hoods mark the award of a university degree or diploma.

Alb

The world 'alb' simply means 'white.' The alb is a fitted white robe with sleeves which may be worn by servers or, at a Communion service, by the minister.

Stole

A stole is similar to a scarf, but coloured according to the season of the Church's Year. It is worn over an alb by a priest or deacon at Holy Communion, Weddings and (often) Funerals.

Chasuble

This is shaped like a Mexican poncho and, in some churches, is worn over an alb and stole by the presiding priest at Holy Communion.

Cope

The cope is a decorative version of a cloak and is worn on very special occasions, e.g. weddings, services of the word on important festivals, and in processions.

A bishop will often wear a cope, together with a hat called a mitre.

Geneva Gown

This is a long, loose-fitting black gown worn by some Free Church ministers when conducting worship. It may be worn with an academic hood and bands.

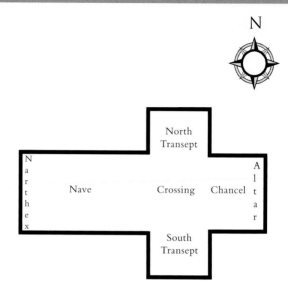

Traditional shape of a church plan

The largest medieval churches were often built in the shape of a cross called a 'Cruciform' shape. Notice how the building 'faces' East – towards Jerusalem.

INSIDE THE CHURCH

Christians are always keen to point out that a 'church' is not a building, but a group of people who follow Christ and worship God. The first Christians met to worship in one another's homes. However, it was not long before they were setting up their own buildings for worship. Church buildings have changed a lot through history as Christian worship has developed. Today, we have a wide range of types of church building in Britain. Some date from the Middle Ages, others are much more recent.

The largest of the medieval churches were often built in the shape of a cross (called a 'cruciform' shape) with a Nave, Chancel and two Transepts. Smaller churches from this period have a Nave and Chancel. The Nave (the word comes from the Latin word *navis* meaning ship because, if turned upside down, the nave of a church is ship-like) was the place of the people. In the Middle Ages it was used for lots more than worship. Business was carried out here during the week, and it was a meeting-place for the local community. There were no seats, just an open space.

The Chancel was the place of the priests. Here, they performed the church services, while the rest of the people looked on. Usually, the chancel was separated from the Nave by a Rood Screen (see page 149). Most churches were built to face East, the direction of the rising sun, as a reminder of our faith in Jesus who rose from the dead. The altar, where the Mass was celebrated, was placed against the East wall of the Chancel. To celebrate Mass, the priest would stand with his back to the people.

In the 16th century, new ideas began to affect worship, and these had an effect on church buildings, too. Many screens separating the Chancel and Nave were pulled down and altars (which had been pushed against the East wall of the church) were turned round and placed lengthways in the Chancel. This was to let the people gather round at Holy Communion. The priest was now directed to stand along the (long) North side of the table.

Large numbers of new churches were built in Britain in the 18th and 19th centuries. In the 18th century, worship was very different from how it is today. Holy Communion was celebrated perhaps only three times a year. The main service of the day was Morning Prayer, usually with a very long sermon. For this reason, churches of this period had large pulpits, usually in a central position. The top deck of the pulpit was the only place from which every person in the building could be seen!

In the later 19th century, people began to be interested again in what church buildings had looked like in the past: many later Victorian churches were built in the same style as medieval ones, and lots of older churches were re-built.

There were two big differences, though. The Nave was now usually filled with pews, and the Chancel was usually fitted with a set of choir stalls. Up until the middle of the 19th century, most church musicians had sung and played from a gallery, often at the West end (back) of the church. These 'gallery bands' gave way to robed choirs, most of which sang (to organ accompaniment) from the Chancel.

Altars were usually now bigger than had been the case in the 18th century, and were often built several steps higher than the rest of the chancel. Sometimes, the East end of the Chancel was richly decorated.

In the 20th century, there was a move in all mainstream churches to make Holy Communion the central act of worship each Sunday. The understanding of Communion changed, too – from a service taken by the priest with the congregation looking on, to a celebration in which all God's people share together. To make this clear, many churches moved their altars (or put in new ones) to the front of the Nave, so that everyone could gather around it and be fully involved in what was happening.

Most new church designs from about 1960 have a 'nave altar', and some were even built in a circular shape.

Other changes have taken place in many church buildings in recent years. Some have had pews removed and replaced with chairs, to give more flexible seating and to allow the Nave space to be used for community events other than worship. In many places, the music is now led by an informal music group as well as (or instead of) a choir, and this has often needed space. A growing number of churches now project the words of the service and the hymns and songs onto a screen rather than giving people a service book or hymn book. This has also changed the look of the inside of some church buildings.

THINGS TO LOOK FOR INSIDE
A CHURCH BUILDING

The **Font** is the place where new Christians are baptized. Because baptism marks the entry of a new Christian into the family of the Church, fonts are normally near the church door. In Baptist churches, baptisms take place in a large pool (Baptistry). Baptismal pools have become more common in Roman Catholic and Anglican churches in recent years, as have fonts with running water.

Photo:Ash Mills

The **Altar** (or Holy Table) is a table made of wood or stone on which the bread and wine are placed at Holy Communion. Many churches have more than one altar. One might be at the far East end of the building, another in a small side chapel, and another might be at the front of the Nave (see page 142).

The **Bishop's Seat**. This is usually found only in a Cathedral. Its Latin name *cathedra* is why a cathedral is so-called: it is the main church of a diocese in which the Bishop has his seat. In some places, the bishop's seat is very grand and is known as the 'bishop's throne.' In others, it is more simple. Some large parish churches may also have a special seat for the bishop.

Photo: Ash Mills

The **Lectern** is a special reading desk from which passages are read from the Bible. Often, the back of the Lectern is decorated with an eagle. The eagle is the sign of St John, the writer of the Fourth Gospel, which begins 'In the beginning was the word...' (*John 1:1*)

Pews were added to many parish churches from the 16th century onwards. Many of the early ones were 'box' pews with high sides and doors.

Within pews can often be found **hassocks** (or kneelers). These help the congregation to kneel down to pray.

A **Rood Screen** was found in many churches in the Middle Ages. A 'rood' is another word for the cross on which Jesus was crucified. The purpose of the screen was to separate the Nave from the Chancel. Some old rood screens still exist. In some churches, screens were added in the 19th century.

Candles have had an important part to play in Christian worship. In the Middle Ages, the church would have been full of candles. From the 16th to the 19th centuries, candles were allowed only to provide light to see by. Today, though, we are used to seeing candles on the altar, some churches use candles in procession, and some have a special stand (called a pricket stand) where small candles may be lit as a sign that a prayer has been offered.

Many churches light a **Pascal Candle** every Easter. This is a reminder that Jesus, the Light of the World, is risen from death for ever; it is carried into church on the first service of Easter Day (often at around dawn). It is lit at all services during the Easter season and is then placed by the font for the rest of the year, where it is lit for services of baptism.

The **Cross** is the symbol of the Christian faith. Try and see how many crosses you can find in your local church. The building might be shaped like a cross, there might also be crosses on a screen, above the pulpit, or on the altar hangings (see page 145). Sometimes, the cross is empty (reminding us that Jesus has risen from death), sometimes, the cross is a **crucifix**, with the figure of Jesus on it (reminding us of the death that he suffered for us).

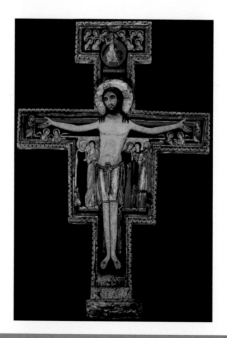

Stained glass can be found in the windows of some churches. In the Middle Ages, all services were in Latin, which only the most educated people could understand. Most people did not read, and so learned about the Christian faith through pictures. Many stained glass windows tell stories from the Bible.

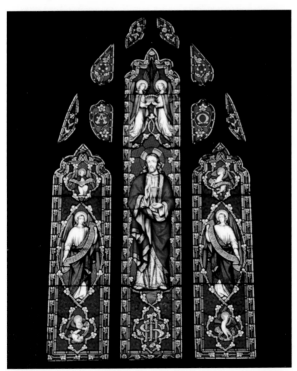

The Nave Organ in Chelmsford Cathedral

THE ORGAN

by Daniel Moult

It is almost certain that the church in which you sing has an organ. The organ is a musical instrument like no other. It is the largest, often the loudest (by far) and certainly the most complicated. It also has one of the longest musical histories behind it. And every organ is very different. Most importantly of all, there is much brilliant music which has been written especially for it.

Many people tend to think of the organ as being a 'church' instrument, but this is not the full story.

If we go back in time, our story begins with the Ancient Greeks who invented a basic type of organ which used water pressure to provide the air to blow through pipes. The Romans used such instruments in theatres and in arenas to accompany chariot fights: the Emperor Nero was said to be obsessed by the organ! It wasn't until many centuries later (probably the tenth century A.D., in fact) that some churches started to install organs.

Nowadays, organs can be found in concert halls, schools, stately homes and even theatres and cinemas, as well as in churches and cathedrals.

How do organs work?

The details are complicated, but the basic facts involve **air** and **pipes**. Nowadays the air is generated by an electric fan, but before the age of electricity the **bellows** had to be pumped manually. Often this job fell to the choristers, and if the organ was large it was very hard work.

All that air is stored in a **box** or **reservoir** and sent through the organ. When a key is pressed, various parts of the mechanism called the **action** (which might be direct and mechanical, or electric, or even pneumatic) open very small trap doors (called **pallets**) under the pipes and allow air into them.

Pipes produce all the different notes of the organ. The ones which you can see are almost certainly just a fraction of the total number of pipes. All of the remaining pipes are inside the instrument in what we call the case.

On an average-sized church instrument, there might be about 800 pipes. You can probably see only about 20 to 50 of those on the front and side of the organ!

The outside of the case might be very decorated and impressive. The insides, though, are often very complex, compact and sensitive (and sometimes dangerous, too). You should never go inside without adult supervision.

The organ at St. Bavo, Haarlem, Holland.

Handel and Mozart have both played the organ at St Bavo. Mozart played it when he was only 10.

If you do venture inside an organ, you will see pipes of all different sizes and shapes.

The taller the pipe, the lower the pitch of the note will be. The shorter the pipe, the higher the pitch will be.

In very large organs, the tallest pipes might be 32 feet high (10.6 metres) which is even higher than 2 double-decker buses, one on top of the other! The smallest pipe is probably about the size of your little finger (and is so sensitive that it would go out of tune if you brushed it lightly when walking past.)

Most pipes are made of metal, although some are wooden and produce softer sounds.

Some pipes look more like metal cylinders. These contain reeds in the boot at the bottom of the pipe, so that the sound is rather like a trumpet or oboe or clarinet, depending on how the pipe is made.

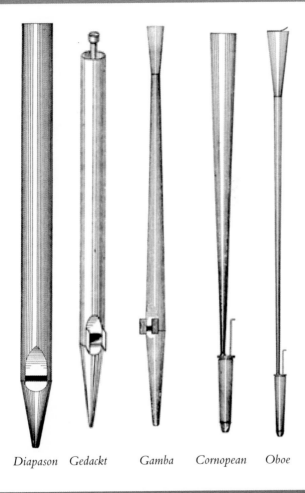

Diapason Gedackt Gamba Cornopean Oboe

The Organ

How can the player (the organist) manage to operate all these hundreds or thousands of pipes? The answer is in groups. Pipes are arranged in groups (mostly 1 pipe per note of the keyboard). These groups of pipes are controlled by **stops** which the organist selects at the side of the keyboards.

The stops might work by being pulled out (**drawstops**) or pushed down (**stop tabs**). Look at the different names which the stops have on the **console** (the keyboards and controls from where the organist plays and makes music).

There are thousands of possible names, some of them foreign, which describe the sort of sound and the type of pipe, e.g.

Principal or Open Diapason	Normal metal pipes making a clear, typical "organ" tone
Gedackt	You won't guess this one! Flutey toned pipes
Gamba	Stringy toned pipes, like smaller, thinner versions of principal pipes
Cornopean	Trumpet toned pipes (one of the sorts of reed pipe mentioned above)
Oboe	These are oboe toned pipes (no prizes if you guessed this one!)

It is possible that your church has an organ without any pipes. Electronic or digital instruments aim to copy something of the unique sounds which a pipe organ can produce.

The number at the bottom of the stops tells the organist the pitch of the notes: 8' means normal pitch (the bottom pipe of the group is 8 feet long), 4' higher pitch (an octave higher than the 8' stops), 16' lower pitch (an octave lower than the 8' stops) etc. By mixing the different pitches and sounds together, there are lots of possibilities even on a fairly small organ with only a handful of stops. Most organs have more than one keyboard or manual for extra possibilities and for extra power (the sounds of the different keyboards can be linked together).

 Organs can have 1, 2, 3, 4 or even 5 manuals (the world's largest organs in the U.S.A even have 6 and in one case 7 manuals!)

If you look down on the floor of the console, you will probably see a keyboard for the feet. These outsized wooden keys, called the pedals, have their own sounds or stops. They provide mostly the bass or lowest notes of the music and need to be played with especially light shoes so that the organist can feel the notes without having to look down too often.

Liverpool Anglican Cathedral Organ Console

Music for the organ

The most famous composer, who wrote superb music for the instrument, is Johann Sebastian Bach.

There are many organ composers who you might have heard of (maybe from singing choral music which they written), such as Byrd, Purcell, Mendelssohn, Liszt, Brahms, Elgar and plenty of more recent and living composers.

As well as for solo playing, in churches the organ is also used to accompany choirs and congregations in anthems and hymns.

Listening to the organ

If you want to see what playing the organ involves and to hear it as a musical instrument, perhaps you might offer to turn the pages of the organist's music after the service? (After all, his or her hands and feet will probably be quite busy as they play!)

You might want to buy some inexpensive single organ tracks off a music website to listen further. Here are just a few suggestions to get you started:

J.S. Bach	Toccata and Fugue in D minor BWV565 (probably the most famous piece of music written for the organ ever.)
F. Haydn	Eight pieces for musical clock (gentle, flutey-toned pieces)
C.M. Widor	Toccata from *Symphonie V* (an exciting work which has also become popular as a wedding piece)
O. Messiaen	Transports de Joie... from *L'Ascension* (a breath-taking modern-sounding piece)
G. Ligeti	Harmonies (this piece creates strange sounds by having the stops drawn out only part-way and by limiting the wind supply to the pipes – fascinating music!)

Learning to play the organ

Perhaps you want to learn the organ? If you're not entirely sure that it's the right instrument for you, you could try booking just a few lessons before you commit to it. As with any musical instrument, it takes a while at first to progress but you will improve if you practice carefully and regularly.

Some organ teachers will take on young people with no or little keyboard experience, whilst others will take on people after about Grade 5 level piano. If you can't find a good, local organ teacher, visit one of the websites below★. There are also websites which can give you more information on all aspects of the organ.

Some websites:

www.agohq.org/guide
www.DanMagic.org
www.oundlefestival.org.uk/organ
www.organschool.com

Mozart called the organ "the king of instruments" – perhaps you might agree with him as you get to learn more about it!

★ correct at the time of writing

CHURCH MUSIC COMPOSERS

ARCHER, Malcolm (b.1952). English organist, conductor and composer. Formerly Organist and Director of Music at St Paul's Cathedral, and now Director of Chapel Music at Winchester College. As a composer, he has a unique gift for composing for parish choirs with over 200 published compositions, including *My song is love unknown*, *Rejoice the Lord is King* and *Prayer of St Richard of Chichester*. In 2009 he was awarded an honorary Fellowship of the RSCM.

ASTON, Peter (1938–2013). University lecturer and composer. He held senior academic posts at the University of York and University of East Anglia, where he taught for twenty five years. His best known choral works include the *Evening Service* in F and the anthem *The true glory*.

ATTWOOD, Thomas (1765–1838). Pupil of Mozart; Organist of St Paul's Cathedral and composer to the Chapel Royal. His many anthems include *Come Holy Ghost* (suitable for Whitsun) and *Turn thy face from my sins*.

BACH, Johann Sebastian (1685–1750). Regarded as one of the greatest composers of all time, Bach's church music includes Passions (St Matthew & St John), the *Mass in B minor* and the *Christmas Oratorio*, as well as over 200 Cantatas for the Church's year. *Jesu, joy of man's desiring* is sung by most church choirs. His organ works provide the basis for every organist's repertory.

BAIRSTOW, Edward (1874–1946). Organist at York Minster for over 30 years, and also Professor of music at Durham University. Many of his works are standard repertoire, including the anthems *Blessed city, heavenly Salem; Save us, O Lord;* and *Let all mortal flesh* and the canticle *The Lamentation of Jeremiah.*

BATTEN, Adrian (1590–1637). Chorister at Winchester Cathedral. Organist of St Paul's Cathedral. Batten was a prolific composer of Evening service music and anthems. The most widely used anthems include *O sing joyfully* and *Lord we beseech thee.*

BERKELEY, Lennox (1903–1989). Was of French ancestry and studied in France before becoming a professor at the Royal Academy in London. Though mainly a composer of instrumental music, he wrote masses, settings of the canticles and anthems for both the Anglican and Catholic liturgy including *Look up sweet babe, Sweet was the song* and *The Lord is my Shepherd.*

BINGHAM, Judith (b.1952). Studied at the Royal Academy in London and won the BBC Young Composer Award in 1977. A composer of orchestral and choral music who combines dissonance with melody, her 13 years as a member of the BBC Singers gave her a deep understanding of writing effectively for singers. She has composed for many cathedrals and for both King's and St John's Colleges in Cambridge including anthems, two settings of the *Magnificat and Nunc Dimittis* and three mass settings.

BLOW, John (1649–1708). Composer and organist. He was appointed organist at Westminster Abbey in 1668 at age 19. In 1674 he became a Gentleman of the Chapel and the same year succeeded Pelham Humfrey as Master of the Children. He was appointed choirmaster at St Paul's Cathedral in 1687. Among his pupils were William Croft and Henry Purcell. *Salvator mundi* is often sung at Passiontide.

BOYCE, William (1711–1779). Widely regarded as one of the most important English-born composers of the 18th century. Boyce was a chorister at St Paul's Cathedral before studying music with Maurice Greene after his voice changed. He was appointed Master of the King's Musick in 1755, becoming organist at the Chapel Royal in 1758. His church music still retains a place in Anglican cathedral repertoire.

BRAHMS, Johannes (1833–1897). One of the great 'Romantic' composers – symphonies, songs, chamber music etc. Some movements from his *German Requiem* are sung as anthems, most notably *How lovely are thy dwellings fair*. One of his most famous orchestral works is a set of *Variations on a Theme by Haydn*, known as the *St Antony Chorale*.

BRITTEN, Benjamin (1913–1976). Lived most of his life at Aldeburgh, Suffolk, where he founded the famous festival. Regarded as the greatest English composer since Purcell. Best known for his operas, including *Peter Grimes*, *Billy Budd* and *Albert Herring*. His church music includes *Rejoice in the Lamb* and *Hymn to the Virgin* (for double choir). The widely-sung

Jubilate in C was written at the request of the Duke of Edinburgh in 1961 as a companion to his *Te Deum in C* published nearly thirty years previously.

BRUCKNER, Anton (1824–1896). Best known for his orchestral symphonies, he was for most of his life a regular organist at the Monastery of St Florian in Austria (where he is buried under the organ) and at the Cathedral in Linz. His Mass settings are large scale works, and his unaccompanied Latin motets are sung widely by cathedral and parish choirs, especially *Locus iste, Christus factus est, Virga Jesse* and *Os justi*.

BYRD, William (1542–1623). One of the most respected Renaissance composers; he shared the post of organist to the Chapel Royal of Queen Elizabeth I with Thomas Tallis. Despite religious intolerance, he remained a Roman Catholic and much of his church music is in Latin. He was loyal to the Queen who recognised his genius and tolerated his Catholicism. Byrd's vocal sacred and secular works alone fill 19 volumes and he also left many keyboard pieces. The three *Masses* (for 3, 4 and 5 voices), his *Evening Services* and motets such as *Ave verum Corpus, Sing joyfully* and *Justorum animae* are widely sung.

CHILCOTT, Bob (b.1955). A former member of the King's Singers is an international choral conductor and composer who specialises in writing for young voices. His church music ranges from very simple gentle carols such as *Mid-Winter* through the rhythmically exuberant *Nova! Nova!* and *A Little Jazz Mass* to an 8-part arrangement of the *Tallis Canon*.

CROFT, William (1678–1727). Was a chorister at the Chapel Royal under John Blow and in 1708 he succeeded his master as organist of Westminster Abbey where he was eventually buried. His well-known *Burial Service* has been used for many royal and other state funerals. He composed around 75 anthems, some organ music and the hymn tunes *St Anne* and *Hanover* are also attributed to him.

CROTCH, William (1775–1847). Was said to have been able to play *God Save the King* on the organ at the age of two and to have given an organ recital before the King at the age of four. He studied in Oxford and was organist of Christ Church Cathedral at the age of 15. In 1822 he became the first Principal of the Royal Academy of Music in London. His oratorio *Palestine* was once popular and *Lo! Star-led chiefs* from this is often sung at Epiphany. *How dear are thy counsels* is another anthem that remains popular.

DARKE, Harold (1888–1976). Studied with Stanford and served as organist at St Michael's, Cornhill in London for 50 years during which time he gave around 1800 lunch-time organ recitals. He deputised for Boris Ord at King's College, Cambridge during the war years. He is perhaps best known for his carol *In the bleak mid-winter*, his *Evening Service in F* and for three *Communion Services*. He also composed some notable organ music.

DURUFLÉ, Maurice (1902–1986). Parisian organist of Saint-Etienne-du-Mont, he was badly injured in a car crash and had to give up playing in 1975. A notable teacher, he was a perfectionist who published very few pieces. These were mostly for organ, but his *Requiem* and *Ubi caritas et amor* from *Quatre Motets sur des Thèmes Grégoriens* are very well known.

DYSON, George (1883–1964). A pupil of Stanford, he served in the First World War and was musical director of the RAF. He taught in public schools (Marlborough, Rugby, Wellington, Winchester) and became Principal of the Royal Academy of Music in 1937. Knighted in 1941, his *Evening Services in D, F and C minor* are widely used.

ELGAR, Edward (1857–1934). One of England's greatest 20th Century composers, Elgar began his musical career as organist of St George's Roman Catholic Church in Worcester, though he was himself a violinist. After his symphonies, concertos, chamber music, oratorios such as *The Dream of Gerontius* and the orchestral *Enigma Variations*, church music forms only a small proportion of his output; but his simple early motets, especially *Ave verum*, are much loved by parish choirs and the large scale anthems *Give unto the Lord* and *Great is the Lord* by larger choirs. His anthem *The Spirit of the Lord*, an extract from the oratorio *The Apostles*, is also widely sung and his organ *Sonata* is one of the finest of its time.

FARRANT, Richard (d.1580). Born in either 1530 or 1540, he was a Gentleman of the Chapel Royal (that is 'a singer'), joint-organist of St George's Chapel in Windsor from 1564 and also Master of the Chapel Royal from 1569. He composed morning and evening services and the anthems *Call to remembrance*, *Hide not thou thy face* and *When as we sat in Babylon* (one of the first 'verse anthems'). The anthem *Lord, for thy tender mercies sake* used to be attributed to him, but is now thought to be the work of John Hilton (c.1560–c.1608).

FAURÉ, Gabriel (1845–1924). Although we now regard Fauré as a great composer, he struggled for recognition in his own time and earned so little from his compositions that he needed the income from his posts as choirmaster and organist to Parisian churches to survive. He eventually became director of the Paris Conservatoire in 1905. His *Requiem* and *Cantique de Jean Racine* are firm favourites.

GIBBONS, Orlando (1583–1625). Served at the Chapel Royal through the whole of the reign of King James I and was also organist of Westminster Abbey for the last two years of his life. Recognised as one of the greatest musicians of his time, all his church music has English texts: his *Short* and *Second Services* and anthems such as *Hosanna to the Son of David, O clap your hands* and *O Lord, in thy wrath*. He was a pioneer in writing verse-anthems such as *This is the record of John* and *See, see the Word is incarnate*. His hymn tunes, known as *Songs*, such as *Song 1, Song 13* and *Song 34* still feature in most hymn books. Very little of his music was published in his lifetime.

GREENE, Maurice (1695–1755). Was a chorister at St Paul's Cathedral under Jeremiah Clarke, and he became organist there himself in 1718. He was also Master of the King's Musick, a founder of the Society of Musicians and he began a project to compile a large collection of church music for all the cathedrals in the country. He died just before this was finished, but the collection was eventually published as "*Boyce's Cathedral Music*" in 1756. His own anthems include *Thou visiteth the earth* for harvest, and *Lord, let me know mine end.*

GUERRERO, Francisco (1528–1599). A Spanish Renaissance composer, he was a chorister in Seville Cathedral and became choirmaster at Jaen Cathedral by the age of 17. From 1555 he was back in Seville and, after visiting the Holy Land in 1589, he was captured by pirates and held for ransom. He composed both sacred and secular vocal music which includes over 150 *motets*, over 20 *masses* and several *Passions*. His music has a special spiritual quality and his *Ave virgo sanctissima* of 1566, is one of the best-known Spanish works of the 16ᵗʰ Century.

HANDEL, George Frideric (1685–1759). Was born in Germany but lived in London from 1712 until his death. A prolific composer, he composed over 40 operas, 29 oratorios including *Messiah*, many cantatas, arias, and duets, 16 organ concertos, 16 keyboard suites, much chamber music, two sets of *Concerti Grossi* for orchestra and a great deal of sacred music. His music was often written for special occasions, such as *The*

Fireworks and *Water Music*, and the anthem *Zadok the Priest* has been performed at every Coronation since the ceremony for King George II and Queen Caroline in 1727.

HARPER, John (b.1947). Was a chorister at King's College, Cambridge, and organist of Birmingham RC Cathedral and Magdalen College, Oxford. He was then Professor of Music at the University of Wales, Bangor and Director General of the RSCM from 1998 to 2007. Mainly a composer of liturgical music, he has published a unison *Mass for all Seasons*, *The Welsh Eucharist*, a setting of *The Chorister's Prayer* and several anthems.

HARRIS, William (1883–1973). Known as 'Doc H' to his choristers, he was organist of New College and Christ Church, Oxford before his appointment to St George's Chapel, Windsor in 1933. He conducted at the Coronations of 1937 and 1953 and was knighted in 1954. Of his eight double-choir anthems, *Faire is the heaven* and *Bring us, O Lord God* are especially fine. Smaller anthems of note include *Holy is the true light* and *Behold, the Tabernacle of God*, the latter composed for the dedication of the Chapel in Addington Palace, former home of the RSCM. His *Evening Services* in *A* and *A minor* are still sung in cathedrals and his hymn tune *Alberta*, written on a railway trip across Canada, is in several hymnbooks.

HARVEY, Jonathan (1939–2012). Was a chorister at St Michael's, Tenbury, and studied in Cambridge, Glasgow and Paris. A composer who used electronics in his music and was once called 'The English Stockhausen'. He wrote church music alongside his major orchestral works and operas and was awarded an honorary Fellowship of the RSCM in 2000 for his services to church music. His best known anthems are *I love the Lord* and *Dove descending.*

HARWOOD, Basil (1859–1949). Was organist of Ely Cathedral and of Christ Church Cathedral, Oxford. When his father died in 1909 he retired to live in Gloucestershire to manage the family estates but Harwood went on composing until the age of 87. He left a *Service in A flat* (Morning, Evening and Communion), the anthem *O how glorious is the Kingdom* and some popular hymn tunes such as *Luckington, St Audrey* and *Thornbury.*

HAYDN, Franz Josef (1732–1809). Austrian composer, known as the 'Father of the Symphony' because he composed 104 of them, was a chorister in Vienna for nine years but was dismissed when his voice changed. He had no training as a composer and taught himself from text-book. He worked for the Esterházys for more than 30 years and it was at the end of this time that he composed his great Masses (including the so-called *Nelson* and *Harmonie* Masses) and the two oratorios *The Seasons* and *The Creation,* the latter work from which the well-known chorus *The heavens are telling* is taken. The exciting motet *Insanae et vanae curae* started life as a 'storm' chorus in an oratorio and was later reworked by Haydn to this new text.

HOLST, Gustav (1874–1934). Studied with Stanford at the Royal College of Music where he became lifelong friends with fellow student Vaughan Williams. He taught at St Paul's Girls' School and Morley College in London and is best known for his orchestral suite *The Planets*. It is from this that the hymn tune *Thaxted* (*I vow to thee my country*) is taken. Holst composed and arranged a number of carols including the popular tune *Cranham* for *In the bleak mid-winter* and his arrangement of *Personet Hodie*. His *Hymn of Jesus* is a fine cantata for choir and orchestra.

HOW, Martin (b.1931). Was a student at the RSCM when based in Canterbury after World War II. He then served as Choirmaster and Headquarters Commissioner to the RSCM at Addington Palace in Croydon and he inaugurated the RSCM Southern Cathedral Singers. A specialist in training young people and a composer who understands the limitations of parish choirs, he designed many of his numerous works to be flexible in their use. He has composed many settings of the *Evening Canticles* and *Communion Service* and his *Parish Communion Service* was widely used during the Church of England's 'ASB' years. His setting of *The Chorister's Prayer* is notable along with the anthems *Day by day, Fairest Lord Jesus* and *Praise, O praise*.

HOWELLS, Herbert (1892–1983). Was a pupil of Sir Herbert Brewer at Gloucester Cathedral and then studied at the Royal College of Music in London where he later taught for over 50 years retiring in 1972. He was one of the most important and influential composers in 20th Century English Church Music with a total of 20 sets of *Evening Canticles* and 9 of *Morning Canticles* to his credit, composed over a period of 58 years for specific locations. The *Collegium Regale* canticles for King's College, Cambridge, are perhaps his most well-known along with the four anthems (including *Like as the hart* and *O pray for the peace of Jerusalem*) and the three carol-anthems (*Here is the Little Door*, *A Spotless Rose* and *Sing Lullaby*).

IRELAND, John (1879–1962). Studied at the Royal College of Music with Stanford and served as organist of St Luke's in Chelsea for over 20 years. His compositions include *Services* (in *F* and *C*), the fine anthem *Greater love hath no man*, a short anthem *Ex ore innocentium* (written for one of Sydney Nicholson's wartime chorister courses) and the hymn tune to *My song is love unknown*, supposedly written in 15 minutes on a scrap of paper when the hymn text was suggested to him. He also published several organ pieces.

IVES, Grayston (b.1948). Grayston 'Bill' Ives, a former member of the King's Singers, held the unique title of Informator Choristarum at Magdalen College, Oxford until retiring in 2009. Composer of several canticles, communion services and over 25 anthems including *Listen, sweet dove* and *There is a land of pure delight*, as well as lyrical Christmas carols *Sweet was the song* and *O remember Adam's fall*. He was awarded an honorary Fellowship of the RSCM and a Lambeth Doctorate in 2008 for his services to church music.

JACKSON, Francis (b.1917). Was a chorister at York Minster under Sir Edward Bairstow and returned there to succeed his teacher as organist in 1946, serving until retirement in 1982. His compositions include much organ music, canticles (the *Evening Service* in G, *Benedicite* in G and *Communion* in G being the best known) and many anthems. His hymn tune *East Acklam* (sung to *For the fruits of His creation*) is included in many contemporary hymnbooks.

JACKSON, Gabriel (b.1962). Was a chorister at Canterbury Cathedral and studied at the Royal College of Music in London. His choral music, much of it very simple in construction, is mostly meditative and spiritual. Many cathedrals and major choirs have commissioned works from him including an *Evening Service*, a *Mass*, a set of *Preces and Responses* and many published anthems. Another side of his personality can be heard in his *Rhythm and Blues* for saxophone quartet.

JOUBERT, John (b.1927). Originally from Cape Town in South Africa, he came to study in London in 1946 and went on to teach at Hull and Birmingham universities, retiring in 1986. In 1952 he won a competition run by the publisher Novello with his anthem *O Lorde, the maker of al thing* and this was followed by the popular carols *Torches* and *There is no rose*. He is also the composer of two symphonies, three concertos and much instrumental and organ music.

JOSQUIN DES PRES (c.1440–c.1521). Sometimes written as Josquin Despres or simply Josquin, his name in Flemish means 'Joseph of the fields'. He was the first great Renaissance composer of polyphonic music and, unlike many composers, he was extremely famous in his own time. Many of his compositions survive including at least 15 masses, 60 motets and 60 songs. The best known mass is the *Missa de Beata Virgine* and perhaps the most famous of his songs is a short humorous song *El Grillo* (*The Cricket*).

LANGLAIS, Jean (1907–1991). Blind organist of the Basilica of Sainte Clotilde in Paris for over 40 years. Although a prolific composer and noted improviser, he was best known as a teacher who influenced and inspired several generations of young French, American and British organists. Organ music and sacred liturgical music form the bulk of his 254 opus numbers and of his 13 masses the *Messe solennelle* is widely sung in cathedrals.

LASSUS, Orlandus (1532–1594). A Flemish Renaissance composer sometimes called Orlando di Lasso, he was as famous in his day as Josquin and even more of his works survive. These include 60 masses, 540 motets and over 400 songs and madrigals. From 1556 he worked mainly in Germany where he was a popular and influential teacher.

LEIGHTON, Kenneth (1929–1988). A former chorister of Wakefield Cathedral, he studied at the Queen's College, Oxford and was a pupil of Bernard Rose, Edmund Rubbra and Goffredo Petrassi. He taught at the universities in Leeds, Edinburgh and Oxford before his appointment as Professor of Music at Edinburgh University. His powerful anthem *Solus ad victimam*, astringent *Preces and Responses*, angular *Evening service* for Magdalen College, Oxford, poetic setting of the *Coventry carol* and athletic *Let all the world in every corner sing* are all widely admired, as is much of his organ music.

LINDLEY, Simon (b.1948). Studied at the Royal College of Music in London. Secretary of the Church Music Society and a past president of the Royal College of Organists, he has been organist of Leeds Minster since 1975 and also Leeds City Organist. His beautiful setting of *Ave Maria* is a firm favourite with many choirs along with carol arrangements such as *The Bell-Man's Song*, *On Easter morn* and *Now the green blade riseth*, all for Eastertide.

LLOYD, Richard (b.1933). A former chorister at Lichfield Cathedral, he was organ scholar at Jesus College in Cambridge. Following a spell of National Service, when he qualified as a tank gunner, he subsequently served as organist of Hereford and Durham Cathedrals. His descants, church and organ music are widely published and well known. They include several sets of responses, evening canticles for Hereford and Salisbury cathedrals and many anthems. Best known of these is the beautifully prayerful motet *View me, Lord*, composed whilst he was assistant organist in Salisbury in 1963.

MACMILLAN, James (b.1959). A Scottish composer who came to prominence in the 1990's with a concerto based on *Veni, veni, Emmanuel* for percussionist Evelyn Glennie. A committed Catholic, he has written music for the liturgy, including mass settings for congregation, a series of *Strathclyde Motets* and a cantata *Seven Last Words from the Cross*. Among his anthems and motets, *A New Song* widely popular.

MATHIAS, William (1934–1992). A major Welsh composer and, although he wrote in many musical genres (including eleven concertos), his organ and choral works are a significant part of his output. Educated in Aberystwyth and at the Royal Academy of Music with Lennox Berkeley, he was Professor of Music at Bangor University and he founded the North Wales Music Festival at St Asaph Cathedral. His anthem *Let the people praise thee, O God* was composed for the marriage of Prince Charles and Lady Diana Spencer and 750 million people heard the first performance. His anthems *Let all the world in every corner sing*, *Lift up your heads*, a *Missa Brevis* and several carols are also well-known.

MENDELSSOHN, Felix (1809–1847). German composer and child prodigy who gave his first piano recital when he was nine and by the age of 14 he had composed 12 symphonies. He was popular in England and made several visits here. A London friend, William Bartholomew, translated his oratorio *Elijah* into English and commissioned him to write *Hear my prayer* with its famous solo *O for the wings of a dove*.

Several anthems in cathedral and parish repertoire are extracts from his oratorios including *There shall a star*, *Above all praise and majesty*, *I waited for the Lord* and *How lovely are the messengers*.

MERBECKE, John (c.1510–c.1585). Often spelt Marbeck or Marbecke, was a lay clerk and then organist of St George's Chapel in Windsor. He was arrested with two other lay clerks and condemned to death for heresy in 1544 but reprieved by the Bishop of Winchester and returned to his organist duties. He is best known for his *Book of Common Prayer Noted* of 1550, a complete setting of the new English services to plainsong using the principle of a single note to each syllable. This remained in use for over 400 years but its use declined with the arrival of the ASB and *Common Worship* services.

MOORE, Philip (b.1943). Was organist of Guildford Cathedral and then, for more than 25 years at York Minster until retirement in 2008. His portfolio covers a wide spectrum, from Liturgical music (17 settings of the *Evening Canticles*, 14 *Communion/Mass settings* and 5 sets of *Responses*), through over 120 anthems and carols to full scale cantatas and a Passion. His beautiful Passiontide anthem *It is a thing most wonderful* was composed for an RSCM festival and his *Preces & Responses*, *Three Prayers of Dietrich Bonhoeffer* and his plainsong based *Evening Services* are in the repertoire of many churches and cathedrals.

MONTEVERDI, Claudio (1567–1643). In his nine books of Madrigals, Monteverdi began a transition from the Renaissance style of music to the Baroque. He composed 18 operas of which the first, *Orfeo* 1607, is regarded as the first serious opera ever written. His *Vespers* of 1610 was his first sacred work and contained sections for soloists and some for choir. From 1613 he directed the music at San Marco in Venice and in 1632 he became a priest. Most of his church music comes from this later part of his life including the motet *Beatus vir* and several masses.

MORLEY, Thomas (c.1557–1602). His life events are a little uncertain. He was probably a chorister at Norwich Cathedral and served as organist there (1583-1587). Possibly a pupil of William Byrd, he may have served as a Gentleman of the Chapel Royal from 1592 and may have either sung or played at St Paul's Cathedral c.1591. Best known as a madrigalist and composer of church music, he also wrote *A plaine and easie introduction to practicall musicke*. His evening services and the anthems *Let my complaint*, *Out of the deep* and *Nolo mortem peccatoris* are often sung. The last of these is interesting in that it combines Latin and English texts.

MOZART, Wolfgang Amadeus (1756–1791). Austrian composer and one of the greatest composers of all time, beginning at the age of five and completing over 600 works before his death at the age of 35. Despite his fame he died in poverty. His symphonies, operas, chamber, church and instrumental music are all highly regarded and his motets *Ave verum corpus* and *Laudate*

Dominum are widely sung in church along with several of his *Missae Breves*.

NICHOLSON, Sydney (1875–1947). Sir Sydney was organist of Carlisle and Manchester Cathedrals before appointment to Westminster Abbey in 1919. He founded the School of English Church Music in 1927 incorporated by Royal Charter as the Royal School of Church Music in 1945, and worked tirelessly to teach and train choirs and organists in both the UK and around the world. He served as music editor to *Hymns Ancient & Modern*, contributing tunes to several editions. He was responsible for the *Parish Psalter* and composed anthems and services suitable for both parish and cathedral. He was knighted by King George VI in 1938 for his services to church music. He is buried in Westminster Abbey.

OGDEN, David (b.1966).   Studied at Bristol University, was Director of Music at Clifton Cathedral from 1991 to 2002. He directs the RSCM Millennium Youth Choir and is a Special Advisor to the RSCM. His anthems, all contemporary but tonal, include *Go forth and tell*, *Christ has no body now but yours*, and *Love's redeeming work is done*.

OUSELEY, Frederick Arthur Gore (1825–1889). The Revd Sir Frederick Ouseley founded the College of St Michael in Tenbury, a choir school which sang Anglican cathedral style services from 1865 until closure in 1985. He was Precentor of Hereford Cathedral and Professor of Music at Oxford University to whom he left his unique library of rare books, manuscripts and music. His anthems include *O Saviour of the world* and *From the rising of the sun*.

PALESTRINA, Giovanni Pierluigi da (1525–1594). Italian composer and choirmaster in Rome and regarded as one of the greatest composers of choral music in his time and a great influence of the composers that followed. His technique of writing voice parts is still taught today. He left over 100 masses and around 500 other vocal pieces including madrigals, numerous motets, Magnificats and other liturgical music. His masses are still sung, the best known being *Missa Aeterna Christi Munera*, *Missa Brevis* and *Missa Papae Marcelli*.

PARRY, Charles Hubert Hastings (1848–1918). Sir Hubert Parry was a major figure in the British musical scene around the turn of the century. He was the director of the Royal College of Music, was knighted in 1898 and became Professor of Music at Oxford in 1900. He was one of the first British composers to write *Chorale Preludes*, organ music based on hymn tunes. His double choir anthem *I was glad*, a setting of Psalm 122, has been sung at every Coronation since 1902. His seven motets *Songs of Farewell* and the setting of John Milton's Ode *Blest pair of sirens* are often sung and his hymn tunes *Jerusalem*, *Repton* and *Laudate Dominum* are very well known, the last two being taken from larger works.

PITONI, Giuseppe (1657–1743). From the age of 20 until his death, he was choirmaster at San Marco in Rome, also serving at St Peter's Basilica from 1719.

Nowadays we think of him as a 'one piece' composer, remembered for his short anthem *Cantate Domino*, but his compositions number 3500, almost all sacred music. They include 325 Masses, c.800 Psalm settings and 236 motets.

POULENC, Francis (1899–1963). French pianist and composer belonging to a group of modern composers called 'Les Six'. Best known for his instrumental and orchestral works, which include a famous concerto for organ, he composed church music, notably a *Mass in G, Salve Regina* and *Quatre motets pour un temps de pénitence* followed in 1952 by *Quatre motets pour le temps de Noël*.

PURCELL, Henry (1659–1695). Said by many to be the greatest English composer of all time, he was organist of Westminster Abbey from the age of 21 until his death also serving simultaneously at the Chapel Royal from 1682. He developed an individual style of English Baroque music which was different to that prevailing in Italy or France. Composer of operas including *Dido and Aeneas*, a vast amount of instrumental music, songs, theatre music, a complete *Service in B flat*, an *Evening Service in G minor* and around 80 anthems including *Rejoice in the Lord alway* (the *Bell* anthem), *They that go down to the sea in ships*, *Jehova, quam multi sunt, Hear my prayer* and *Remember not, Lord, our offences* to name but a few. Many of these have solo verses and use strings as well as organ. He composed *Funeral Music for Queen Mary* for her funeral in 1695 and a few weeks later it was used for his own funeral.

ROSE, Bernard (1916–1996). Was organist in turn of The Queen's College and Magdalen College, Oxford except for war service during which time he was held prisoner-of-war. An eminent scholar and editor of the music of Thomas Tomkins, he is best known for his *Preces & Responses*, perhaps the first modern set of responses to win widespread acclaim and acceptance.

RUTTER, John (b.1945). One of the leading composers for the church in recent decades. From his very first published work, *The Shepherd's Pipe Carol* written as an undergraduate student in 1966, his ability to craft melody to words with an understanding of good vocal line has ensured that his music is much loved by singers and audience alike. His anthems, carol and folk-song arrangements are too numerous to mention but include *A Clare Benediction* and Harvest anthems *All things bright and beautiful* and *Look at the World*. The anthem *I will sing with the spirit* was composed for the RSCM in 1994 using our motto for its text. His *Requiem* is popular worldwide and received a very large number of performances in the USA after the tragic events of 9/11.

SCHUBERT, Franz (1797–1828). Austrian composer of nine symphonies, 600 Lieder (songs), much chamber and instrumental music together with church music in the form of seven *Masses* and around 30 liturgical pieces. His upper voice setting of *The Lord is my Shepherd* is popular, both in its original form and as an SATB arrangement.

SCHÜTZ, Heinrich (1585–1672). Worked from the age of 30 in Dresden and was one of the most important German composers before Bach. Nearly all his music (over 400 pieces) is sacred and naturally most is in German or Latin. Amongst the more popular motets are *Jauchzet dem Herrn* and *Jubilate Deo* together with the last movement from his *St Matthew Passion* using the English text *Praise to Thee, Lord Jesus*.

SHAW, Martin (1875–1958). Organist in London of St Mary's in Primrose Hill, and of St Martin-in-the-Fields, he was a founder member of the Plainsong & Medieval Music Society and the Purcell Society. A friend of Vaughan Williams, he helped in the editing of the hymn book *Songs of Praise* and *The Oxford Book of Carols*. His *Anglican Folk Mass* was much sung before the introduction of the ASB and *Common Worship* liturgies. His hymn tunes *Little Cornard* and *Marching* are still much used.

SHEPHARD, Richard (b.1949). A former chorister at Gloucester Cathedral and pupil of Sumsion, he was a lay clerk in Salisbury Cathedral Choir and headmaster of the Minster School in York. His *Addington* and *Wiltshire* Communion services were amongst the first and most popular when the new ASB services were introduced. His many fine anthems include *Holy is the true light*, *The secret of Christ*, *Out of the stillness* and *Ye choirs of new Jerusalem*. His setting of the Easter Exultet, *Sing choirs of heaven*, and *Preces and Responses* are both widely used.

STAINER, John (1840–1901). A chorister at and later organist of St Paul's Cathedral, he was also Professor of Music at Oxford University. Although his other music fell out of fashion for a time, his cantata *The Crucifixion* has remained popular since it was written in 1887. His *Evening Service* in *B flat* and double choir anthem *I saw the Lord* both remain in the repertoire of many large choirs and *God so loved the world* (from *The Crucifixion*) and *How beautiful upon the mountains* are still widely used along with some of his hymn tunes.

STANFORD, Charles Villiers (1852–1924). Studied in Cambridge and Germany, organist of Trinity College in Cambridge from 1873 to 1892 and Professor of Music at Cambridge University from 1887 until his death. One of the most important Anglican church musicians although church music formed only a small part of his career. He taught many notable musicians at the Royal College of Music in his 41 years as professor there and he himself composed operas, concertos, chamber music, seven symphonies and six *Irish Rhapsodies*. His organ music, including five sonatas in Germanic style, is very fine. His *Evening Services* (especially those in A, B flat, C, and G) are widely used as are the *Three Motets* and the anthems *Ye choirs of new Jerusalem*, *The Lord is my shepherd*, and *How beauteous are their feet*. In a 1998 survey of cathedral music his *Beati quorum via* (from the *Three Motets*) and *O for a closer walk* were in the 'top ten' of all anthems sung.

SUMSION, Herbert (1899–1995). Organist of Gloucester Cathedral for almost 40 years, conductor of the Three Choirs' Festival and composer of church and organ music. His five *Evening Services* (three in G – SATB, boys and men and two more in D and A), *Benedicite* in B *flat* and *Te Deum* in G are all justifiably popular along with the anthem *They that go down to the sea in ships*.

TALLIS, Thomas (c.1505–1585). A Gentleman of the Chapel Royal, he was also joint organist there with Byrd. Like Byrd, he wrote both Latin and English church music which is much admired 450 years later and his Responses and Litany are still in use. His settings of the *Lamentations*, the amazing 40-part motet *Spem in alium* for eight 5-part choirs and the evening *Short Service* are acknowledged masterpieces. The anthems *O nata Lux* and *If ye love me* are sung in many parish churches and *Audivi vocem*, *In ieiunio et fletu* and *Salvator mundi* in many cathedrals.

TAVENER, John (b.1944). A direct descendant of the Tudor composer John Taverner, he joined the Russian Orthodox Church in 1977 and has written for the orthodox and Anglican liturgies with his *Collegium Regale* service for King's, Cambridge. He was a friend of The Beatles who recorded his *Requiem* on their 'Apple' label. His setting *The Lamb* is often used as a Christmas carol and his *Song for Athene* was used at Princess Diana's funeral.

TAVERNER, John (c.1490–1545). Whilst organist of Christ Church, Oxford he was arrested for heresy but, like Merbecke, pardoned for 'being but a musician'. He then gave up music and moved to Boston in Lincolnshire as landowner, businessman and civic official. Most of his music is for the Latin pre-reformation liturgy and is regarded as a link between the early 15th century John Dunstable and the late 15th century Thomas Tallis. Of his eight mass settings, the *Western Wynde Mass* and *Mean Mass* are the most popular and *Dum transisset sabbatum* (for Easter) is his best-known anthem.

TIPPETT, Michael (1905–1998). Conductor and composer was knighted in 1966, in WWII he was imprisoned as a 'conscientious objector'. He wrote operas, symphonies, chamber music and the very successful oratorio *A Child of our time* from which his popular and richly scored settings of *Spirituals* are taken. He was not a religious man and only set one liturgical text, the spectacular *Magnificat and Nunc Dimittis* for St John's College, Cambridge.

TOMKINS, Thomas (c.1572–1656). Welsh born organist of the Chapel Royal and also simultaneously of Worcester Cathedral, serving there for 60 years. His music was published after his death by his son as *Musica Deo Sacra*, a collection containing five services, 95 anthems (both verse anthems and full anthems) and some madrigals. His *Preces and Responses* are much used. One of the later Tudor composers, his music is more expressive than some of his predecessors, notably the anthem *When David heard that Absalom was slain*.

VAUGHAN WILLIAMS, Ralph (1872–1958). A student of Parry and Stanford at the Royal College of Music, composer of nine symphonies, concertos and other orchestral music, film and ballet music. A collector of folk-songs, he arranged some of these into hymn tunes as Editor of *The English Hymnal*, *Songs of Praise* and *The Oxford Book of Carols* and these remain very popular. He was such an important composer that he is buried in Westminster Abbey near to Purcell and Stanford. His church music includes a *Mass in G minor*, a Communion motet *O taste and see* (written for the Coronation in 1953), a *Te Deum in G*, large scale anthems such as *O clap your hands, Lord, thou hast been our refuge* and the exuberant *Let all the world* from his *Five Mystical Songs*.

VICTORIA, Tomas Luis de (1548–1611). Spanish composer but spent much time in Rome and so his name is sometimes spelt the Italian way – Vittoria. He was a contemporary of Palestrina but his music is more homophonic than Palestrina's and uses more dissonance to achieve expression. His masses *O quam gloriosum*, *O magnum mysterium* and matching motets with the same titles, together with pieces from his *Holy Week Tenebrae,* are especially notable.

WALFORD DAVIES, Henry (1869–1941). A chorister at St George's Chapel in Windsor, he was organist of the Temple Church in London for 25 years. Knighted in 1922, he gave many lectures on BBC Radio and was Master of the King's Musick for the last seven years of his life. He composed many anthems, introits and services but is most remembered for the *RAF*

March Past, *Solemn Melody*, for the carol *O little town of Bethlehem* and for his timeless chant setting of *Psalm 121*.

WALMISLEY, Thomas Attwood (1814–1856). Professor of Music at Cambridge University from the age of 22, he was organist of three Cambridge Colleges simultaneously which led to very busy Sundays! Although he wrote nine services, only those in B flat, D and D minor are regularly sung today. The D minor *Magnificat and Nunc Dimittis* is especially fine and is one of the first settings to have a fully independent organ part. Apart from these, his short choral hymn *From all that dwell below the skies* and a few Psalm chants are still in use.

WALTON, William (1902–1983). A former chorister at Christ Church Cathedral, Oxford, he was mainly self-taught as a composer and is best known for his orchestral music and film scores. The short anthem *A Litany* was written when he was a 15 year old student. His other church music includes the wedding anthem *Set me as a seal upon thine heart*, a *Missa Brevis*, *Jubilate Deo*, a *Magnificat and Nunc Dimittis* for Chichester Cathedral, a few carols and the substantial anthem *The Twelve*.

WEELKES, Thomas (c.1575–1623). Organist of Chichester Cathedral for the last 21 years of his life, described as a 'lively character' his behaviour led to trouble with the cathedral authorities. A noted composer of madrigals with four books published in his lifetime, he left nine evening services and many excellent anthems including *Hosanna to the Son of David*, *Gloria in excelsis Deo* and *Alleluia! I heard a voice*.

WESLEY, Samuel Sebastian (1810–1876). Son of Samuel Wesley and great-nephew of John Wesley, the founder of Methodism, he was a notable figure in the development of church music in the mid 19th century. He was outspoken in his views and not an easy man to get on with. As a result he held posts in many places, often not staying for very long, including four churches in London, Leeds Parish Church and four cathedrals – Hereford, Exeter, Winchester and Gloucester. His wonderful anthems are justly popular as indeed is the *Evening Service* in E. His *Blessed be the God and Father* has been in the top ten anthems of several surveys, with *Thou wilt keep him in perfect peace* and *Wash me throughly* not far behind. His large scale anthems including *The Wilderness*, *Ascribe unto the Lord* and *Praise the Lord, O my soul* are more demanding, although *Lead me Lord*, the final section of the last mentioned, is both easy and popular.

WILBY, Philip (b.1949). Studied at Keble College in Oxford, and was a violinist in the Birmingham Symphony Orchestra before teaching at Leeds University. For much of his life also a church organist, his works include both straightforward parish music such as *God be in my head*, *Make me a light* and *If ye love me* as well as more complex pieces such as *Vox Dei* and the *Trinity* and *St Paul's* services. In 2009 he was awarded an honorary Fellowship of the RSCM.

WILLCOCKS, David (b.1919). A former chorister at Westminster Abbey, he was organist of Salisbury and Worcester Cathedrals before appointment to King's College, Cambridge where he succeeded the Boris Ord and served for 26 years, enhancing the worldwide recognition of the choir there through his recordings and through broadcasts of the Christmas Eve Carol service. A distinguished choral conductor, he was co-editor of the *Carols for Choirs* series of anthologies and is perhaps best known to singers for his truly memorable carol arrangements and descants.

WOOD, Charles (1866–1926). Like Stanford, he was of Irish birth. He studied with Stanford in Cambridge and succeeded him as Professor of Music there. He worked with The Revd G.R.Woodward to produce several carol books including *The Cowley Carol Book*. His popular arrangements include *Ding, dong! merrily on high* and *This joyful Eastertide*. Along with Howells, he has composed more sets of evening canticles than any other composer – there are 20 settings, of which those in D, E flat and the *Collegium Regale* set in F are the best known. His anthems include *O Thou, the central orb*, *Oculi omnium*, *Expectans expectavi*, *Glorious and powerful God*, *Great Lord of Lords* and the unaccompanied double-choir anthem *Hail, gladdening light*.

COMPOSER TIMELINE

Moments in History	Composers
1066 Battle of Hastings	Peter Abelard 1079–1142
1086 The Domesday Book is compiled	Hildegard of Bingen 1098–1179
1100 William Rufus is killed by an arrow while hunting in the New Forest	Leonin 1135–1201
1170 Thomas Becket is killed in Canterbury Cathedral	Perotin 1160–1205
1189 Richard I (the Lionheart) becomes king	
1215 King John seals Magna Carta	
	Guillaume de Machaut 1300–1377
1340 Geoffrey Chaucer is born	
1348 The Black Death comes to England. Perhaps a third of the population died over the next year.	
1381 The Peasants Revolt. Peasants in Essex and Kent rise up and march on London. The king manages to persuade them to disperse by making promises, none of which he intends to keep	

Composer Timeline

	John Dunstable 1390–1453
	Guillaume Dufay 1397–1474
	Gilles Binchoise 1400–1460
1453 The Hundred Years War ends. England loses all its territory in France except for Calais	Josquin des Prez 1440–1521
1455–1485 England suffers a series of civil wars known as the Wars of the Roses	
1476 Caxton introduces the printing press into England	
1485 Henry VII wins the battle of Bosworth. Richard III is killed and Henry becomes the first Tudor king	
	John Taverner 1490–1545
1497 John Cabot sails to North America	Thomas Tallis 1505–1585
1509 Henry VIII becomes king	
	John Merbecke c.1510–1585
	Andrea Gabrieli 1510–1586
	Giovanni Pierluigi da Palestrina 1525–1594
	Francisco Guerrero 1528–1599
1533 Henry divorces Catherine of Aragon. He marries Anne Boleyn	Orlando di Lasso 1532–1594

1534 Henry VIII makes himself head of the Church of England	
1536–1540 Henry VIII closes the monasteries and confiscates their property	William Byrd 1542–1623 Tomas Luis de Victoria 1548–1611
1549 An Act of Uniformity imposes a Book of Common Prayer	 Giovanni Gabrieli 1553–1612
1555–1558 Queen Mary persecutes Protestants. Nearly 300 people are burned to death for 'heresy'	Thomas Morley 1557–1602
1558 Queen Mary (also known as 'Bloody Mary') dies. Elizabeth I becomes queen	 Claudio Monteverdi 1567–1643 Thomas Tomkins 1572–1565
1576 The first theatre opens in London	Thomas Weelkes 1575–1623
1577–1580 Francis Drake sails around the world	
	Orlando Gibbons 1583–1625
1588 The Spanish Armada is defeated	Heinrich Schütz 1585–1672 Adrian Batten 1590–1637
1605 The gunpowder plot, a Catholic conspiracy to blow up parliament, is discovered	

1611 The King James Bible is published	
1642 Civil war between king and parliament begins	
1649 King Charles I is beheaded	John Blow 1649–1708
1653 Oliver Cromwell becomes Lord Protector of England	
	Guiseppe Pitoni 1657–1743 Henry Purcell 1659–1695
1660 Charles II becomes king	
1665 Plague in London. This is the last outbreak of bubonic plague in England	
1666 The great fire of London. Most of the city is destroyed but it is soon rebuilt	
1673 The Test Act is passed. Catholics and Protestant dissenters are prevented from holding public office	
	William Croft 1678–1727 Antonio Vivaldi 1678–1741
	George Frederick Handel 1685–1759 Johann Sebastian Bach 1685–1750

1694 The Bank of England is founded	Maurice Greene 1695–1755 William Boyce 1711–1779
1721 Robert Walpole becomes the king's main minister. People call him the Prime Minister. (Originally it was a term of abuse)	
1735 The Prime Minister moves into 10 Downing Street	Franz Josef Haydn 1732–1801
1739 John Wesley founds the Methodists	
	Wolfgang Amadeus Mozart 1756–1791 Thomas Attwood 1765–1838
1773 The Stock Exchange is founded	
1775 Jane Austen is born	William Crotch 1775–1847
1783 Britain signs a treaty recognising the independence of the American colonies	
1787 The first convicts leave Britain from Portsmouth for Australia	Franz Schubert 1797–1828
1799 Income tax is introduced to pay for the war against France	
1805 The battle of Trafalgar	

1807 The slave trade is abolished	Felix Mendelssohn 1809–1847 Samuel Sebastian Wesley 1810–1876 Thomas Attwood Walmisley 1814–1856
1815 The battle of Waterloo	
1821 John Constable paints *The Haywain*	Anton Bruckner 1824–1896
1825 The world's first public passenger railway opens (The Stockton and Darlington railway)	Frederick Ouseley 1825–1881
1829 The Catholic Emancipation Act gives Catholics civil rights	
1832 The Great Reform Act is passed. Seats in parliament are distributed more fairly and the middle class are given the vote	
1833 Slavery is abolished throughout the British Empire	Johannes Brahms 1833–1897
1837 Victoria becomes queen	
	John Stainer 1840–1901
1842 A new law bans women and children from working underground in mines	Gabriel Fauré 1845–1924
	Hubert Parry 1848–1918

1851 The Great Exhibition is held in London	Charles Villiers Stanford 1852–1924
1854–1856 The Crimean War is fought. Britain and France defeat the Russians	
1857–1858 The Indian Mutiny takes place	Edward Elgar 1857–1934
1859 Darwin publishes The Origin of Species. It outlines his theory of evolution	Basil Harwood 1859–1949
1863 The first (steam driven) underground train in London	
1865 The Salvation Army is formed (it does not get its name until 1878)	Charles Wood 1866–1926 Henry Walford Davies 1869–1941
1870 Education Act to provide state education for all	
1871 The Bank Holiday Act is passed. (For most working class people bank holidays are their only paid holidays)	Ralph Vaughan Williams 1872–1958
	Gustav Holst 1874–1934 Edward Bairstow 1874–1946

1875 A law bans the practice of sending small boys up chimneys to clean them. From now on you have to be over 21 to clean a chimney that way	Sydney Nicholson 1875–1947 Martin Shaw 1875–1958 John Ireland 1879–1962 George Dyson 1883–1964 Harold Darke 1888–1976
1890 The first electric underground trains run in London	Herbert Howells 1892–1983
1899–1902 The Boer War is fought	Herbert Sumsion 1899–1995 Francis Poulenc 1899–1963
1901 Queen Victoria dies. Her son becomes Edward VII	Gerald Finzi 1901–1956 Maurice Duruflé 1901–1986 William Walton 1902–1983 Lennox Berkeley 1903–1989
1904 Britain signs the Entente Cordiale (friendly understanding) with France	Michael Tippett 1905–1998 Jean Langlais 1907–1991 Benjamin Britten 1913–1976
1914 In August the First World War begins	
	Bernard Rose 1916–1996 Francis Jackson b.1917
1918 The First World War ends in November	David Willcocks b.1919

1922 The BBC is founded	
1926 Workers hold a General Strike but they are defeated	John Joubert b.1927
1928 Universal suffrage is introduced. (Everyone over the age of 21 is allowed to vote)	Kenneth Leighton 1929–1988
1930 Following the Wall Street Crash the depression bites and unemployment rises sharply	Martin How b.1931 William Matthias 1934–1992
1936 George V dies. Edward VIII becomes king but soon abdicates. George VI becomes king	
Television begins in Britain	Peter Aston 1938-2013
1939 The Second World War begins	Jonathan Harvey 1939-2012 Philip Moore b.1943 John Tavener b.1944
1945 Second World War ends	John Rutter b.1945
	John Harper b.1947
	Grayston Ives b.1948
	Simon Lindley b.1948
	Richard Shephard b.1949
1951 The Festival of Britain is held	

	Malcolm Archer b.1952
	Judith Bingham b.1952
1953 Coronation of Elizabeth II	
1954 Food rationing ends	
1955 ITV begins broadcasting	Bob Chilcott b.1955
	James MacMillan b.1959
1962 The Beatles release their first single *Love Me Do*	Gabriel Jackson b.1962
1963 Doctor Who is broadcast for the first time	
1963–65 Dr Beeching axes minor railways	David Ogden b.1966
1967 Colour TV begins	
1969 Capital punishment is abolished permanently	
1971 Britain switches to decimal currency	
1973 Britain joins the EEC (forerunner of the EU)	
1978 The first test tube baby is born	Tarik O'Regan b.1978

CONTRIBUTORS

Harry Bramma
> *Past Director,*
> *The Royal School of Church Music*

John Henderson
> *Hon. Librarian,*
> *The Royal School of Church Music*

Peter Moger
> *Precentor, York Minster*

Daniel Moult
> *Organ tutor,*
> RSCM *Church Music Skills programme*

Leah Perona-Wright
> *Past Manager,* RSCM *Voice for Life programme*

Tim Ruffer
> *Head of Publishing,*
> *The Royal School of Church Music*

ACKNOWLEDGMENTS

We have made every effort to identify all copyright holders of images and to all of them we are most grateful. We apologize if there are errors or omissions and we will correct them in future printings.

Picture Credits

Page 132: The Vicar & PCC of St James' Church, Hampton Hill

Pages 133, 144 & 145: St Mary's Church, Fordingbridge;
Page 148: All Saints' Church, Minstead;
Page 149: Sarum St Martin's &
Page 153: St Martin's Church, Sandford St Martin by Gregor Zednik

Page 141: All Saints' Church, Margaret Street, London.

Page 142: Croydon Minster by Daniel Soper

Page 143: Liverpool Metropolitan Cathedral

Page 144 & 146: Salisbury Cathedral by Ash Mills (www.ashmills.com) are copyright The Dean & Chapter of Salisbury Cathedral

Page 140, 146 & 154: Chelmsford Cathedral by James Norrey

Page 160: Makin Organs Ltd

Page 163: Liverpool Anglican Cathedral

All used with permission and grateful thanks